Living Off the Pacifi floor

Living Off the Pacific Ocean Floor

STORIES OF A COMMERCIAL FISHERMAN

George Moskovita

Oregon State University Press   Corvallis

The paper in this book meets the guidelines for permanence and durability
of the Committee on Production Guidelines for Book Longevity of
the Council on Library Resources and the minimum requirements
of the American National Standard for Permanence of Paper for Printed Library
Materials Z39.48-1984.

Library of Congress Cataloging-in-Publication Data
Name: Moskovita, George, 1913-2004.
Title: Living off the Pacific Ocean floor : stories of a commercial fisherman /
    George Moskovita.
Description: Corvallis : Oregon State University Press, 2015.
Identifiers: LCCN 2015034930 | ISBN 9780870718243 (original trade pbk. : alk.
    paper) | ISBN 9780870717758 (ebook)
Subjects: LCSH: Moskovita, George, 1913-2004. | Fisheries—Northwest, Pacific—
    Anecdotes. | Bottom fishing—Northwest, Pacific—Anecdotes.
Classification: LCC SH221.5.N65 M67 2015 | DDC 639.209795—dc23
LC record available at http://lccn.loc.gov/2015034930

Oregon State University Press
121 The Valley Library
Corvallis OR 97331-4501
541-737-3166 • fax 541-737-3170
www.osupress.oregonstate.edu

Contents

Foreword

Keith Swanson

In *Reader's Digest*, people in a former age read a regular column called "The Most Unforgettable Character"—George Moskovita was one of those. His persona, his personality, his humanity and his sincerity were all undisputed. George's voice also was unmistakable. Sure it was loud—many mused that George did not really need a telephone or any amplification. He had a voice like a megaphone. No one answered his phone calls and asked, "Who is this?" If it was George, you knew right off.

One of his endearing traits (and there were many) was as a storyteller. The family had heard his stories many times.

- Those close calls when he was out fishing in the Pacific or when crossing the ever-dangerous Columbia River Bar
- Boating mechanical problems or breakdowns and the challenges they brought
- Interesting people he had met (or hired) to be part of his crew or merely encountered along the way

He'd start telling one of his favorites—and family members didn't groan or roll our eyes. We wanted to hear it yet another time in his charismatic style and enthusiasm.

He was a pioneer in fishing in Washington and Oregon, but also south to Mexico and north to Alaska.

He was an entrepreneur—always looking for an opportunity to pick up (cheap) a burned-out boat or one that maybe sank at the dock or in shallow waters. "Why in the world did you buy it, George?" his wife June would say. And he would almost always come back with the same reply, "Because I'm the only one in the world who can fix it?" and then he would parenthetically add, "and I think I can make a few bucks on it."

He was, of course, much, much more than that (but that might be another book).

This book came about after having his family asking yet another time why he didn't write a book. Then some members of the family got the idea of writing such a book for him. He said he didn't want to write it down himself. "Okay! But would you at least dictate your wonderful stories onto a cassette and we will take it from there." When that was done, his daughter Jo Ann (Williams) took the tapes and used a Dictaphone to transcribe the stories to computer discs.

My wife Georgene (who died in September 2013) and I (Keith, a son-in-law who has been a family member for fifty years and very close to George) arranged the stories by topic and not by chronology, put them in order by type, and undertook the significant task of editing them, all the while maintaining George's unique style and tone. I admit to editing them somewhat for publication, so you are hearing these amazing stories partly through my interpretation.

The effort was to insure George's voice would continue to be heard—for our children and their children and all those who want to hear and embrace these adventures in early Northwest fishing and history.

So the task began and took several years of work since I mostly used my summer vacation time to write. While I was writing, Jo Ann's husband Charles Williams was scanning the pictures and articles George wanted to use in the book. Eventually he laid out the format of the book for publication. With the exception of a few noted pictures, all are from George's private and extensive collection. He was an avid photographer and a vast many are of fishing, boats, and his catch.

The stories themselves embrace George's sixty-year career as a commercial fisherman, starting when he was a child in Bellingham, Washington, catching Dungeness crabs and selling them door to door. The following years were prime time for commercial fishing. There was an abundance of fish, modern engines and equipment were being produced, and new markets opening up for the fisheries. George pioneered the bottom fish industry in Astoria, Oregon, by being the first to center his career there. Others who had fished there came from, or went to, other ports.

When not fishing, one of his other related occupations was rebuilding boats. Much of this book is about the boats and their equipment. When he began he encountered sailing ships, there were no radio telephones, fathometers, radar, or GPS, and gas or diesel engines were less reliable. George has had more boats sink, some with him on board, than most of us will ever own.

Vacation travel routes ran along the coast, so that every small fishing port could be checked when George and the family traveled from Oregon to Southern California. He once made a cross-country trip to Florida in the summer, with his wife, June, three of the daughters, and the much-loved black cocker spaniel, "Blackie"—all to work on a boat he had heard about.

All together, this is the fascinating story of a Croatian immigrant's son making good in America and shaping local history on the Northwest Coast. So, sit back and enjoy some fascinating reading by listening to George's unique voice through these stories.

George thanks the *Daily Astorian* (previously the *Astorian Budget*) for the use of articles.

Introduction

Carmel Finley and Mary Hunsicker

George Moskovita was sixteen, a member of the crew on his father's salmon boat, the *Elector*, when he first went fishing on the ocean. It was 1929 and he had fished in the calm waters of Bellingham Bay, but as the *Elector* headed past Cape Flattery out of the Strait of Juan de Fuca to seine for salmon off Tatoosh Island in the Pacific Ocean, he got seasick. "'Boy, this is not for me!'" he recalled saying, and then: "But of course it was for me! I didn't know it then, but I was to spend my entire life on that ocean" (15).

Soon he was fishing for salmon in Alaska, sardines off California, and tuna off Mexico. During World War II, he caught sharks for their vitamin-rich livers. He helped pioneer trawling out of the Oregon port of Astoria, where he moved in 1939. He once delivered 150,000 pounds of rockfish to a processor. He saw the fishery he had helped build devastated by foreign processing ships.

George was part of a volatile, dynamic, and risky world in which fishing was being revolutionized. Bigger engines, better refrigeration, continued improvement in trawl gear, and new species of fish catch combined to keep George on the water year-round, from Mexico to Alaska. He owned sixteen boats throughout his career. He "retired" from ocean fishing in 1975 and moved back to Bellingham with his wife, June. George and June gillnetted around Bellingham until 1986 on their 37-foot gillnetter, the *Janeth*, but as George said, he was fishing in Puget Sound, and that "wasn't in the Pacific Ocean so it really doesn't count."[1]

From the beginning, George documented his adventures with black and white photographs and an 8-mm movie camera, recording shark catches during World War II. He played his home movies on a sheet pinned to a wall in his living room; then he narrated what he was doing on a tape recorder. Perhaps he saw how quickly fishing was changing around him. Perhaps he wanted to show June and their four daughters—he named boats after each of his girls, and one boat became the *Four Daughters*—his life at sea. Whatever the motivation, George was a superb storyteller, with a vivid sense of the drama that was happening around him in the fishing world. He was frequently on the front page of the *Daily Astorian* for sinking a boat or trawling up a human skull or an unexploded Japanese bomb.

George's stories are a window into the development of fishing along the West Coast of the United States during the Great Depression of the 1930s and during the post-war boom. Fishing developed over hundreds of years in Northern Europe. But on the West Coast of the United States, development was far more rapid, with fisheries industrializing—and showing signs of collapse—within decades or within a few years, as with Oregon's first fishery collapse, for soupfin sharks (*Galeorhinus zyopterus*).

The west coasts of continents are highly productive for fish stocks—but they can also be highly variable. Strong winds over the ocean churn the sea, bringing colder, nutrient-rich waters from the ocean floor to the surface. This upwelling of critical nutrients stimulates the production of phytoplankton and zooplankton, which form the base of the food chain for larger predators, first sardines and anchovies, then salmon and rockfish. The timing of spawning events of larger fishes coordinates with periods of peak production of small prey fish, which maximizes survival rates of larger fishes. When the winds don't blow, the productivity of this ocean food chain is dampened.

Despite this potential abundance, ocean trawling was slow to come to the northwestern corner of the United States. There were many early efforts, but they ended with the sinking of various boats and the closing of small plants, as recorded in one of the most important primary documents about this period, the 1956 doctoral dissertation by George Yost Harry Jr.[2] Early fisheries were concentrated where there was a population to buy fresh fish, especially around Seattle, San Francisco, and Monterey. Fisheries developed regionally, unimpeded by state, provincial, or international boundaries.

American salmon and halibut boats fished off British Columbia and into the waters of Bristol Bay in Alaska. British Columbian salmon boats fished deep into the waters of the San Juan Islands.[3] American tuna clippers during the 1930s increasingly fished off Mexico, then Peru, Ecuador, and Chile. Fishing boats moved with ease and so did the processing equipment. When fish stocks declined in one area, which often happened rapidly, the equipment could be moved to a new site. As Puget Sound salmon stocks faltered after World War I, processors moved their canning equipment to Alaska.[4] As the California sardine fishery dwindled in the 1950s, the processing equipment was moved to Peru.[5] The fish, the boats, and the processing equipment were all mobile, and so was the capital.

The development of fishing off Oregon was generally instigated with capital from investors outside the region, looking to make high returns on investment. California boats and processors played significant roles in the development of Oregon's trawl and tuna fisheries. Federal money, first as price supports during World War II and the Korean War, helped provide the first steady markets for ocean-caught fish.

Despite low prices and limited markets, the 1930s were a time of expansion of the fishing industry on the West Coast. New technologies to catch fish were spreading rapidly among fishermen. New markets were opening and there were no restrictions on who could buy a boat or a fishing license. Booms were quickly followed by busts and a push to pioneer fishing in new waters. It was the over-fishing of California sardines (*Sardinops sagax caerulea*) during the 1930s that sent Monterey processors and their boats to Coos Bay in 1935, looking for new sources of sardines. Seventy-five California purse seiners made deliveries to four plants that sprang up in Coos Bay and three new plants in Astoria. The Oregon fishery peaked in 1939, with a catch of 22,000 tons.[6] The Monterey boats stimulated the development of commercial fishing in Oregon.[7]

California trawl boats began exploring the waters off Astoria in 1937, looking for new stocks of rockfish and soles.[8] A California sardine boat, the *Robin*, caught a ton of albacore on tuna gear off Coos Bay on August 11, 1936. The tuna was initially shipped to California for processing, but the next year, the Columbia River Packers Association (CRPA) converted the half-pound line in its Astoria cannery to pack tuna, putting two hundred women to work.[9]

The Depression hit everyone hard; for fishermen, it was difficult to find a market that would pay enough to cover costs. Fishing offered opportunities—but the work was difficult and dangerous. "There was no big money to be made in fishing, but you could make a living at it," George wrote (27). Often he did not make much money. A crewman on a good San Diego tuna clipper could make $3,000 a year, but he could just as easily wind up with nothing; that happened on one of George's tuna trips. "It was a bum deal for the crew" (33).

Still, a hard-working young man with no family could make enough to buy a Durant car, and an even snazzier Auburn convertible, hauled from San Pedro to Bellingham on the back deck of the *New Zealand*, the boat his father, Dome Moskovita, had built in 1931 at the Barbee Shipyard in Seattle. It was 56 feet long, the limit that Alaska allowed for purse seine boats to net salmon in its waters. Dome also owned the *Elector*, which he used to crab in Bellingham Bay; he built crab pots for sale to other fishermen.

By 1939, Dome and his two sons, George and his older brother, Jack, were fishing from California to Alaska. The family was based in Bellingham, but wanted to move to a more convenient location. Astoria was ideal—roughly midway between Alaska and California. There were salmon to catch—George writes that his father caught salmon in 1917 near the mouth of the Columbia River. There was the new fishery for tuna and the new processing plant. George brought the *New Zealand* to Astoria, with a load of crab pots and some drag gear. When his father took the *New Zealand* back to Bellingham to fish for salmon, George brought his first boat, the *Treo*, a 55-foot trawler with a gas engine, extremely rudimentary controls, and even more limited safety equipment.

"Since the light Puget Sound crab pots were not satisfactory for use off the Columbia River, Captain Moskovita turned to trawling," wrote George Yost Harry Jr.[10] He recorded that George made day trips, without ice, and fished for one and three-quarter cents per pound, selling to mink farmers who needed a cheap supply of protein. Raising mink for their fur was a $2 million industry in Oregon, with about two hundred mink farms, most of them on the coast. It was dependent on a cheap supply of food, mainly horsemeat but also fish carcasses.

The arrival of the Puget Sound boats was news in Astoria. The October 5, 1940, edition of the *Daily Astorian* ran a picture of George on the front page. He was shown on a boat called the *Trio*, the back deck awash with dogfish (*Squalus suckleyi*), and the caption read, "Many dogfish are taken here." The story briefly noted that the boat's hoist had been damaged picking up the catch.[11] George's catch went to the mink farmers.

Four Puget Sound boats started the trawl fishery off Oregon, Harry wrote: the *Trio, Foster, Rio Janeira* (original spellings), and *New Zealand*. The boats originally made deliveries into Newport. The first substantial landings at Astoria were in 1940, when twenty vessels landed an estimated 2 million pounds of dogfish and another 700,000 pounds of fish food. During 1940, the center of the trawl fishery moved from Newport to Astoria.[12]

Eventually, the New England Fish Company offered George three cents a pound for his fish. "No ice was used, landings were made at night, and the crew did the unloading," wrote Harry.[13] "We went out about four in the morning and came back about seven or eight in the evening to unload," George recalled. "Then we'd go out again the next day if the weather was good" (37). It was a market, but George had to have known that he was pushing the old *Treo* past its limits. In October 1939 the engine's bearings burned up on the way back from the fishing grounds and the boat had to be towed back to port.[14] Just weeks later, the *Treo* hit bad weather on its way home and sank. The dramatic rescue of George and his crew was front-page news.

With the *Treo* gone, George went back to being a crewman on California tuna boats. Once again, he didn't make any money. When the war against Japan was announced in December 1941, he considered joining the military. But fishermen were essential workers during the war, needed to supply fish to a population that increasingly could not find meat to buy. He returned to Astoria in 1942 and entered into a partnership with his father to run the *Electra*. There was a strange boat at the dock in Astoria, with "flags and barrels and anchors and miles of line and all kinds of nets with six-inch glass balls and a whole deck of gear," George wrote (42). The *Tordenskjold* was rigged to fish for soupfin shark. George set to work to mimic the gear on board the strange boat. His girlfriend, June Berg, helped him put caps on empty quart beer bottles to create floats that he tied to pieces of old linen gill nets.[15]

The war in Europe was reaching out and touching American fishermen. After Germany invaded Norway on April 9, 1940, the Nazis diverted all Norwegian food items back to Germany, including all the cod liver oil produced there. Vitamins had not yet been synthesized and the oil was a rare source of vitamins A and D. Most of the oil came from the livers of dogfish shark and soupfin shark. Buyers paid $1 a pound for the oil—and sometimes much more. George describes a winter fishery during the war when he made about $25,000. "We were getting eight dollars a pound for the liver and every fish had five pounds of liver," Moskovita wrote. "That's about forty bucks for each shark" (44).

Oregon shark landings peaked in 1943, with 270,000 pounds landed. The next year, landings sank to 50,000. The market disappeared once scientists learned to synthesize vitamins.[16] The shark fishery ended in 1949.[17] But the high prices had stimulated fishing along the entire West Coast. What scientists and fishermen didn't know then is that soupfin shark, like many other species found along the West Coast, are slow to recover from overfishing. They can live for many decades, are slow to grow, and have low reproductive rates.

The shark fishery was conducted from twenty to two hundred fathom using gill nets on the bottom or the surface of the water. There were fisheries at Astoria, Depoe Bay, Newport, Coos Bay, and Port Orford. Many species were caught: dogfish, basking shark, bonito, mackerel. The diver net fishery took place during the winter between twenty and eighty fathom. The floater fishery took place as far as one hundred miles offshore. Fishing began in April off Point

Conception and reached northward to the Hecate Straits in British Columbia by September or October.[18] For fishermen like George, the shark fishery was an unexpected windfall, with livers fetching unprecedented amounts of money.

The federal government's wartime role boosted state and local economics in other ways. There was money available to expand port facilities. There were wartime contracts, such as the contract to the CRPA in Astoria to build six large wooden barges for the US Maritime Commission.[19] After the war, the cannery opened its own shipyard, turning out dozens of small, graceful boats that were used on coastal rivers from California to Alaska.

The Army greatly stimulated interest in rockfish; it could be filleted and frozen, and it was available in large quantities. By the end of the war, coast-wide landings had reached 33 million pounds.[20] The US Fish and Wildlife Service released a report outlining the opportunities that West Coast fisheries offered for small businessmen. West Coast processors mostly canned fish, but the Service predicted that as the population increased, markets for fresh and frozen fish would be created.[21]

The *Oregonian* pointed out how the military had stimulated the Oregon fishing industry in a story in May 1944. Where the relatively short salmon season (May to September) had dominated fishing in Astoria, now the season was much longer—the shark fishing and new otter trawl fishery both lasted for nine months of the year, and albacore season lasted four months, starting in July. There were nine canneries. The fishermen "pick up the enormous load to one side of the boat at considerable hazard while the craft heels to port or starboard, often in ticklish seas," wrote the *Oregonian*. "These boats have been known to sneak in over the Columbia River bar after four days of fishing with more than 90,000 pounds of fish dipping the rails and decks below water."[22] George did it many a time, as his pictures testify. It took until the end of the war for trawling to finally get established off the Oregon Coast.[23]

There was little regulation of fishery catches; the only limits came from the plants, which would only take as much fish as they could sell. "When we fished we probably dumped 50 percent of the fish overboard because they were too small to fillet. We used four- to five-inch mesh" (132). Today, the total catches of target and non-target species and size limits are strictly regulated and enforced to prevent population depletions. The gear is also more sophisticated, limiting the catch of smaller fish.

The end of World War II is generally seen as marking a turning point in global fishing, setting the stage for the development of the modern industrial fisheries. The technology developed during the war was rapidly transferred to the fishing industry, greatly expanding its ability to catch and process fish. Radar and loran showed fishermen, for the first time, the fish in the ocean beneath them.

One post-war trend that George followed was the expansion into larger and more powerful engines, capable of hauling larger and heavier nets. His first diesel engine came in 1943, when he bought the *Coolidge II*. He fished for tuna seventy miles off Coos Bay. "You couldn't run five minutes in one direction until you saw a school of tuna just boiling on top of the water. They were all over the place. It didn't matter which direction you went, you'd see a school of fish" (48).

Fishing on the West Coast boomed after World War II. The steady markets during the war had allowed many fishermen to invest in newer, bigger boats. During 1945, Newport fisherman Captain Gordon White and a group of investors built the 90-foot trawler *Yaquina*. The bigger boat allowed White to fish farther off-shore, in deeper water, where he found large numbers of a bright red, medium-sized fish that were generally called rockfish. The proper name for these long-jawed rockfish was *Sebastodes alutus*: fishermen called them redfish, rosefish, or just "Rosies."[24] California boats had pioneered a fishery on them in the waters off California. Now, fishermen were finding large quantities of them in the deeper waters off Oregon.

White delivered a load of rockfish to the Yaquina Bay Fish Company in Newport in 1946. The company filleted the fish and sold them into the fresh fish market. Manager Dudley W. Turnacliff thought the fish were similar to East Coast perch and started to label them "ocean perch." The market for Pacific Ocean Perch, or POP, increased slowly, with a million pounds landed at Newport in 1949. By 1955, boats were fishing for POP from northern California to Alaska.[25]

Just as fishing expanded, so did fisheries science. After the war, all of the fish and game agencies along the coast became more professional. They hired research staff and became more systematic in studying marine fish. In April 1948 the Oregon Fish Commission published its first edition of its *Research Briefs*. The Commission's director of research, Donald L. McKernan, laid out five objectives he and his staff would be concentrating on. The main focus was on salmon, but he also spoke of the "vast unknown pelagic fisheries, which lie beyond our present concepts of fishing areas."[26]

One of McKernan's first hires was a young Oregon biologist, George Yost Harry Jr. Harry was born in Portland in 1919. He was graduated from Oregon State with a bachelor of science in Fish and Game Management in 1940 and a master of science in zoology from the University of Michigan in 1941. After he graduated from the School of Fisheries at the University of Washington in 1945, he was hired by the Fish Commission of Oregon in 1947. Harry was stationed at the field office in Astoria. His first employee was Sigurd J. Westrheim, who would go on to study Rosies as his thesis research.[27]

Another significant development was the building of the *John N. Cobb* in 1950. The 93-foot wooden boat was operated by the US Fish and Wildlife Service and based in Seattle. For the next fifty-eight years, until it was retired in 2008, the *Cobb* played a central role in the development of fisheries science and oceanography in the Pacific.[28] The *Cobb* was attached to the Exploratory Fishing and Gear Research Base in Seattle, operated by the US Fish and Wildlife Service. Its job was to help fishermen find more fish and catch them more efficiently. Fisheries science during this period is marked by its cooperation with fishermen, with all concerned seeking to increase the catch as much as possible.

Fishing was still difficult and dangerous, and it still didn't pay a lot of money. The cost of gear and labor increased and plants still limited how much a boat could deliver. In 1952, trawlers formed the Fishermen's Marketing Association, based in Eureka, to help find markets for their fish.[29]

George made a business out of buying, repairing, and re-selling boats. "I loved the challenge of buying something and rebuilding it or fixing it up and selling it" (93). In the early days, George headed to sea with rudimentary, improvised gear on his own boats. He frequently pushed himself and his crew, as well as his boats. If the boats weren't fishing, they weren't making any money.

He was always quick to jump on a new opportunity. During the fall of 1950 and the spring and summer of 1951, the California Department of Fish and Game conducted explorations for pink shrimp (*Pandalus jordani*) off California. They found commercial quantities of shrimp and boats began to make deliveries of the small pink cocktail shrimp. California lent its trawl gear to the Oregon Fish Commission, and during the fall of 1951, research began, using the new US Fish and Wildlife research vessel, the *John N. Cobb*.[30] It was a heady and exciting time for rapidly growing staff at the state fishery agencies.

George and the *New Hope* entered the shrimp business in 1957. More adventures followed. He was fishing on the *Mary R* in 1965 when it sank off Cape Disappointment, Washington. Nobody was hurt. He continued to buy, renovate, and re-name boats.

The world of Oregon trawling was changing. With the signing of the Peace Treaty with Japan in 1951, the Japanese began to rapidly industrialize their fishing and whaling in the northern Pacific Ocean and Bering Sea. In 1960, a fleet of Soviet factory processing ships began appearing in the Gulf of Alaska. Several hundred feet long, capable of staying at sea for months at a time, the factory trawlers revolutionized fishing. Their large engines were capable of hauling nets that could fish on the sea floor, rolling over large piles of rock and the tall spires of sea mounds that provide habitat for so many fish and invertebrate species. In particular, the big Soviet processing ships caught large quantities of Rosies. POP catches skyrocketed, reaching more than a billion pounds in the Gulf of Alaska in 1965, with a similar fishery peaking off British Columbia the next year.

The boats continued to head south, reaching the waters off Washington and Oregon in 1966. They caught an estimated 35 million pounds in that first year, but the catches dropped quickly. The boom was almost over. The stocks were hit hard, and so were the local fishermen. Between 1967 and 1969, the catch per hour of fishing declined by 45 percent.[31] Despite the almost fifty years since the Soviet fishery, POP stocks have not recovered off Oregon, although there has been recovery off Alaska.

In 1962, the Bureau of Commercial Fisheries began a research program to process low-cost fish into a protein powder that they hoped could be used to alleviate hunger, especially in poor countries.[32] As part of the process, in 1966 it built an experimental plant at Aberdeen, Washington. George's was one of boats that supplied Pacific hake, or whiting (*Merluccius productus*). With more modern technology, George thought the plant would have been a big success. "Back then they couldn't catch enough hake to keep the plant going. After a few years they junked the plant" (133).

George was starting to slow down. He had spent much of his life at sea, leaving June and his four daughters behind him. He bought another boat, a 37-foot wooden gillnetter, and with either June or daughter Kathy Jo by his side, he went back to the fishery where he had started, gillnetting in Bellingham Bay. Being George, he was not finished having adventures. One night the net got snagged on the boat's propeller. "I couldn't steer with the rudder, and I had to steer with a pole and bucket over the side of the boat," George wrote (128). He was towed into Blaine's harbor.

George had a heart attack in 1983 while he was fishing. "The wind was blowing and I was drifting out from the shore. The net was kind of tangled and I was in a big hurry to get it untangled and overboard before I got too far away from the beach. Suddenly I lost my breath. I had to stop and sit down. I knew there was something wrong" (130). He finally quit fishing in 1986 at the age of seventy-three.

Reflecting on George's life and career, Charles W. (George's son-in-law) writes: "George, like all of us, was a part of the natural world and he knew toward the end of his life that the fisheries he helped develop were not sustainable. He had seen it firsthand and I am confident he would be pleased to see his experience and book being used to teach a new generation. What better legacy could a person want?"

As George himself put it, "I don't really miss the fishing. It was a nice way to make a living, you know, but nowadays it's really dog-eat-dog—a lot of competition and lots of headaches involved with the fishing business. I am glad to be out of it. But I was in it a long time and I have a lot of memories of all the things that happened. It has been quite a life. And that's the way it was" (133).

Notes

1   Lee Makovich, "Moskovita, a man for all seasons," *Fisherman's News*, November 1994, 21.

2   George Yost Harry Jr., "Analysis and History of the Oregon Otter Trawl Fishery, 1884–1961," Doctoral dissertation, University of Washington School of Fisheries, 1956. http://ir.library.oregonstate.edu/xmlui/handle/1957/16899, downloaded March 1, 2013.

3   Lissa K. Wadewitz, *The Nature of Borders: Salmon, Boundaries, and Bandits on the Salish Sea* (Seattle: University of Washington Press, 2012).

4   Charles Gilbert and Henry O'Malley, Special Investigations of Salmon Fishery in Central and Western Alaska, Alaska Fisheries and Fur Industries, Document 891, 1919, 143–160.

5   Gregory Cushman, The Lords of Guano: Science and Management of Peru's Marine Environment, 1800–1973, PhD dissertation, University of Texas at Austin, 2003.

6   George Yost Harry, Jr., Oregon Fish Commission Briefs, August, 1948.

7   Janet Gilmore, *The World of the Oregon Fishboat: A Study in Maritime Fishlife*, (Ann Arbor: UMI Research Press, 1986), 42.

8   George Yost Harry Jr., "History of the Oregon Trawl Fishery, 1884–1961," Research Briefs, Oregon Fish Commission, 9 (1), May, 1963, 5–26, 8. http://ir.library.oregonstate.edu/xmlui/handle/1957/16899, downloaded March 1, 2013.

9   Irene Martin and Roger Tetlow, *Flight of the Bumblebee: The Columbia River Packers Association and a Century in the Pursuit of Fish* (Long Beach, WA: Chinook Observer Publishing Company, 2011).

10   Harry, 5.

11   "Many dogfish are taken here," *Daily Astorian*, October, 5, 1940, 1.

12   Harry, 13–15.

13   Harry, 9.

14   "Three fishermen rescued as trawler Treo goes to bottom off Peacock Spit," *Daily Astorian*, December 2, 1940.

15   George and June were married August 20, 1943, in Bellingham. June was born on June 11, 1918, in Moorehead, Minnesota, the daughter of Norwegian immigrants. She was two years old when they moved to Astoria.

16   Sigurd J. Westrheim, "The Soupfin Shark Fishery of Oregon," Research Briefs, Oregon Fish Commission, 3 (1), September 1950.

17   Fishery Statistics of Oregon, Oregon Fish Commission, Contribution No. 16, September, 1951, 11.

18   Fishery Statistics of Oregon, Oregon Fish Commission, Contribution No. 16, September 1951, 10.

19   Irene Martin, 197.

20   *Commercial Fisheries Review*, Vol. 8, No. 10, October, 1946, 4.

21   Fishery Market News, Vol. 6, No. 8, "Opportunities for small business in the fisheries of the Pacific Northwest and Alaska," 2–7.

22   *Oregonian*, "Fishermen in Astoria look to lucrative catches at sea," May 16, 1944.

23   Harry, 16.

24   Bob Hitz, http://carmelfinley.wordpress.com/2012/09/11/how-pacific-ocean-perch-got-its-name/, downloaded March 2, 2013.

25   Dayton Lee Alverson, *Race to the Sea*. (Seattle: University of Washington Bookstore Press), 53.

26   Research Briefs, 1948.

27   Westrheim's (1958) MS thesis included a pioneering analysis of the age and growth pattern of Pacific ocean perch using scales and established that they were far older and slower-growing than anyone had suspected. http://carmelfinley.wordpress.com/2012/09/08/jergen-westrheim-and-rockfish/?relatedposts_exclude=989, downloaded March 2, 2013.

28   http://www.noaanews.noaa.gov/stories2008/20080813_cobb

29   html http://www.trawl.org/, downloaded March 5, 2014.

30   Alonzo T. Pruter and George Yost Harry Jr., "Results of Preliminary Shrimp Explorations off the Oregon Coast," Research Briefs, Fish Commission of Oregon, 4 (1) December 1952, 12–30.

31   Gunderson, Donald R. "Population Biology of Pacific Ocean Perch (*Sebastes alutus*) Stocks in the Washington-Queen Charlotte Sound Region." Dissertation, University of Washington, 1975.

32   Michael L. Weber, *From Abundance to Scarcity: A History of US Marine Fisheries Policy* (Washington, DC: Island Press, 2002), 27.

Prologue

In 1940, I bought my first boat, the *Treo,* out of Poulsbo, Washington, a 55-foot gas trawler. I started dragging with it out of Astoria, Oregon. We had rope gear without any winches. The pilothouse had no controls. We just had a bell. We'd ring the bell for a guy down in the engine room to put the engine in gear or stop it or back it up or whatever we wanted. It was a very old-style system.

There were a lot of dogfish around at that time. We were able to load up with dogfish and did fairly well with it. It was December and we were fishing off Klipsan Beach when it started to blow. When we got to Peacock Spit, near the entrance buoy for the Columbia River, we decided we'd better go back in before it got too bad.

It started blowing even harder. We hit one big swell. She went way up and came down pretty hard so I told one of the guys, "Go take a look in the engine room and see what's going on." He went

down and came back and said, "Gee, there's water right under the floor boards." I rushed down to take a look myself and then yelled, "Hey man, we're sinking!"

Since it was a gas engine, I drained about an inch of gasoline into a bucket and took it back on the stanchion in the stern and lit a match to it. It was raining and blowing, but the flame coming out of the bucket made a pretty good flare. You could see it for a long way. And, by golly, a boat was coming. It was the *Washington*, skippered by Captain John Lampi out of Ilwaco. He saw the gasoline burning and came up and said, "What's wrong?" I said, "We're sinking." He asked, "What do you want to do?" "Well," I said, "I don't want to let the boat go. We're going to try to bail her out." We didn't have any centrifugal pumps, only a hand pump. So we tried to bail her out with buckets, but that didn't work.

We decided we would try to get in, so he started towing us into the river, and, by golly, the towline broke. We started hollering as the boat started filling up pretty fast. We hollered as loud as we could, but it didn't do any good because he couldn't hear us, it was blowing and raining so hard. It was then about midnight. Finally we just saw his mast light. That's all we could see. I knew we were going down so I got out the life preservers. I put my arms through the straps in one, but it fell to pieces and dropped to the deck. They were old and rotten. We should have had better survival gear, but even if we would have realized the condition of what we had, we didn't have any money to buy any. So we had to use what we had. So, it was looking pretty grim on the deck of the *Treo*.

Then all of a sudden, we saw red and green lights. The *Washington* was coming toward us again. He got to us and threw a line which all three of us on board grabbed a hold of at the same time and we jumped overboard. By the time he pulled us over to his boat and got us on board, the *Treo* had gone under.

The next day there was a big write-up in the paper about our trawler, *Treo Goes to the Bottom Off Peacock Spit*. That was December 2, 1940. I lost everything when that boat went down.

↩

On Coxcomb Hill in Astoria is the Astoria Column, or as we locals call it, the Astor Column, with steps inside, all the way to the top. From that observation deck, one has a fabulous view of the magnificent Columbia, the Pacific, and the river bar where I lost the *Treo*.

Astoria is at the mouth of the Columbia River, as it empties into the Pacific Ocean, the end of the Lewis and Clark Trail. These are among the most treacherous waters in the world. Nearly two thousand vessels have been lost near here over the years, some of them mine. Much of the next fifty-five years was spent in Astoria where I lived and centered my life as a commercial fisherman, from Alaska to Mexico. It has been a very interesting life. The ocean is big and when you shine a spotlight into the water at night, it is unbelievably alive. It produces a wealth of food, but when you drag the ocean bottom, you never know what you are going to find in your nets as you pull them in.

What follows are my memories, the pictures of my life, stories about some of the boats I have lost, and some of the close calls and interesting experiences I have had as I went to sea in search of various kinds of fish using a variety of methods to catch them.

ASTORIA, OREGON, TUESDAY, DECEMBER 3, 1940   PRICE FIVE CENTS

THREE FISHERMEN RESCUED AS TRAWLER TREO GOES TO BOTTOM OFF PEACOCK SPIT

Three Saved In Treo Sinking

Captain William Lampi, owner of the Ilwaco troller Washington, is shown standing back of the three men he saved Monday night from the sinking Astoria trawler. Treo. Seated, from left to right, are Captain George Moskovita, owner and skipper of the Treo, David Willis, engineer, from Camas, Wash., and Harry McPeak, cook, from Portland. They are shown on the deck of the Washington at the port docks. A-B photo.

Vessel Which Rescued Three

The 57-foot Ilwaco trawler Washington, owned and skippered by John Lampi, which saved the crew of the Astoria trawler Treo from certain death on Peacock spit Monday night. The Washington was the last boat to enter the river. Visibility was poor and no other vessel was in position to render aid even if the distress signals could have been sighted. A-B photo.

2nd Boat Pulls 3 From Sea

55-Foot Treo Takes Plunge

Astoria's new shark fishery suffered its first loss Monday night when the 55-foot trawler Treo, one of the "high boats" of the fleet, sank in a heavy sea off the southwest edge of Peacock spit.

Captain George Moskovita, owner and skipper of the former Seattle purse seiner, David Willis, engineer and Harold McPeak, cook, were picked up by the Ilwaco trawler Washington as the boat sank under their feet about 10 o'clock Monday night.

Moskovita said the Treo was inbound with a small quantity of fish when Willis, the engineer, found water gushing into the hold. The skipper dished gasoline in a deck bucket set it ablaze for a flare. When the gasoline was burned out, Moskovita was unable to get more fuel from the fast filling engine room. He was unable to ignite oil for another flare.

Other Boat Attracted

Flickering the mast light, Moskovita attracted the attention of the trawler Washington, which was to the south of the Treo, also inbound. The Treo's skipper said he afterwards learned that the Washington was disabled herself with ignition trouble. As soon as her skipper Captain John Lampi, made repairs he rushed to the Treo and asked Moskovita if he wanted to come aboard.

Anxious to save his boat, Moskovita persuaded the Washington to put out a tow line. Maneuvering in the severe chop out to the edge of the spit, the Washington bumped the crippled Treo, but succeeded in taking the boat in tow.

Roadside Council To Be Formed

Not only will Mrs. Jessie M. Honeyman, president of the Oregon Roadside council, be down tomorrow for the organization meeting of a Clatsop county branch but ac-

2500 U. S. Aircraft In Britain

LONDON, (UP)— An estimated 2,500 United States-built aircraft of all types have already been delivered here and are taking part in the life-and-death battle of Britain. Of the 2,500 planes, nearly have

CHAPTER 1
The Shaping of a Life

I am Captain George Moskovita. I grew up on the docks of Bellingham, Washington, with my brother, Jack.

Dad had come to Bellingham from the Island of Vis in Yugoslavia, just north of Dubrovnic. He came about 1910, leaving Vis for the new world and avoiding the army. He came by ship and stopped at Melbourne and Sydney, Australia, and then on to Auckland, New Zealand. He got a job there digging resin before he continued on to the United States.

He stopped at San Francisco and then went on to Alaska to work in a gold mine for a time. He then settled in Bellingham,

Agnes and Dome Moskovita with Jack and George at Bellingham, Washington.

Washington, and married my mother, Agnes Rooney. She was Irish. She came from Lisburn, Ireland, not far from Belfast. My dad fished for salmon in 1917 near the mouth of the Columbia River. He was paid in gold from a bag the skipper carried with him (a bodyguard with a gun went along for protection). Then he went back to Bellingham and worked at the Bloedel Donovan Lumber Mill where he made a couple dollars a day. It wasn't much to support a family. He made some crab rings at home, took them down to the dock one day, baited them with clams, and threw them off the dock, just for something to eat. He caught more crabs than the family could eat, so he began to give them away. Then he wondered if he could sell them. Not only *could* he sell them, he made more money selling crabs than he made working at the mill, so he quit his job, started making his own crab pots with steel frames wrapped with chicken wire, with tarred trap web for the tunnels. He bought a boat, and built a little shack out on some logs to cook the crab.

My mother and father separated when I was about eleven. Jack and I stayed with Dad and he raised us.

Every morning we had to get up before light. My brother and I took turns cooking breakfast. We always had the same thing. We would buy a large loaf of white bread the day before. Then we would stand it on end and slice it from end to end, six slices out of a loaf. We had a wood stove and a wire mesh toaster. We'd hold a slice of the bread over the stove until it was toasted, then turn it over and do the other side. When it was my turn to cook I would sometimes burn one of the slices of bread. That would always be my brother's piece. When he cooked, I would get the burnt piece. My dad always got a good piece. All we had before we went down to the dock was coffee and two slices of this bread with butter. My dad cooked some of the time. He made a good stew. He'd always buy good meat, and we ate well. But he would say to us, "Don't eat all meat. Eat the bread." I can still hear him in his Yugoslav accent.

The float shack Dad built on the logs was tied up to a road made of planks on pilings. It was on the way to Bellingham Sash and Door, which was right at the bottom of the cliff below where the Bellingham post office is now. When we got down to the dock, Dad would go to his 24-foot open crab boat, which had a one-cylinder, two-cycle gas engine. It couldn't have been over 5 or 10 horsepower. He left us at the shack while he went out in Bellingham Bay to pick his crab pots.

Inside there was an old cookstove. We would throw a few small pieces of wood into the stove and fire it up. It had a copper boiler that just fit the top of it. It would hold about three and a half dozen crabs. While our dad was pulling his pots (but before we could go to high school), we had to get the water boiling. Then we'd take off for school.

He would go about a mile offshore. The Dungeness crabs were thick out in the bay. He had about fifty pots tied to one ground line with a buoy on each end. He pulled each of the pots by hand, picked out the crabs, re-baited it with fresh clams, which he had in a 26-ounce tomato can. (We had taken an old file, sharpened to a point, and punched holes in the can so the smell of the clams would come out). The whole process took about an hour.

Every morning I was late to school, so I had to get an excuse from the office. Every morning it was the same thing: "Why are you late?" "I had to work." Pretty soon they would see me coming late again and they didn't even ask. They would just write out the "excuse" and I would go to class.

By the time Dad came in from fishing, the water in the boiler would be ready, so my dad could just throw the crabs in to cook. When school was out at 3:10 P.M. we had to head right back to the crab shack. Then we had to "shake the meat" out of the crabs. We had a galvanized washtub in the shack. We put a 2 x 12 board on the top of the tub. Then we'd hit the crab with a wood mallet and shake the crabmeat into a meat pot and let the shells fall into the tub. I would be on one side and my brother on the other. We'd shake about six to twelve pounds of crabmeat every day.

When I was a boy we mostly worked. I didn't have the chance to play a lot or get into sports. I had to work. There was a store called the S. S. Sakamoto. It was a variety store owned by a Japanese man. Once in a while Jack and I would go in and buy marbles to play with. But, most of the time I worked with the crabs and the salmon. It was all I knew.

On the way in from the bay, my dad would always pick up a log or a timber that was floating in the water. He would hook onto it, and tow it behind the boat back to the shack. With a seven-foot crosscut saw, my brother and I would saw up those logs. He also got a lot of car sticks. These were 6 x 6's, so the logs wouldn't roll off the flat cars. They cast the car sticks overboard when they were unloading the logs. So Dad would bring these in too. This provided enough wood for the cookstove at the crab shack as well as heat for the house. We never bought any fuel.

We sold the crabmeat for fifty cents a pound or the whole crabs three for a quarter. The larger ones would be two for a quarter. After school we'd sell them around town. On Saturdays, since we didn't have to go to school, we'd sell crabs on the streets of Bellingham. We went around to the garages. There the mechanics would buy them to go with their beer. We'd just walk in and ask if anyone wanted to buy some crab. It was a pretty good seller.

Dad had a 1921 Ford, with a box on the back of it. In the summer, when my brother and I were not in school and the crab season was over, Dad would buy salmon from the Pacific American Fisheries. He filled the back end with salmon and at five o'clock we'd go down to the Bloedel Donovan Lumber Mill, right before quitting time. We would have the tailgate down and spread out about ten or twelve *Humpy* salmon right across the tailgate. We sold those salmon to the workers on their way home for thirty-five cents for a whole fish. If that was too much, we'd cut one in half, guts and all, and sell each half for twenty cents. Somebody would want the head, and somebody else would want the tail portion. We did a land-office business for about fifteen minutes until everybody went home. Then we went home, too.

We used to go out in the country and take orders from farmers. Some wanted to can salmon, so we'd take their order and bring them back as much as fifty pounds. We'd always deliver.

My brother would go on one side of the road and I'd go on the other. One day, at a house on my side of the road, I saw a woman looking and nodding her head at me. I thought I had a sale, so I dashed up to the house. She called for me to come into the house. A big window had fallen down on her fingers. The window was too big and heavy for her to lift by herself, so she was trapped there. She couldn't move and her hands were full of blood. I lifted the window up so she could get her fingers out. As I lifted it up and took the pressure off her fingers, she screamed terribly. It must have been really painful. It was lucky we had come by. I don't know how long she had been there, maybe for hours. We called for help and some people came and took care of her.

One summer my dad was out fishing and my brother and I were left alone. He left his 1921 Ford at home, so one day I took it out. I took my friend and his dog. Of course, I didn't have a license. I started out and was just a couple of blocks from home when I had a wreck. My dad used to let me steer the car once in a while, so I felt I knew something about it. What I didn't know was about stopping! So I bent the axle in the wreck. When my dad came home we had to get it fixed. It cost about twenty five to thirty dollars.

The Sunrise Cafe was right by the dock. It was on the corner of Holly where the bridge goes down to the Sash and Door Building Supply. The Ritz Hotel was right across the street. Beside the cafe were some To-Go laundries and S. S. Sakamoto's Variety Store. We used to wash dishes for the Japanese cook at the Sunrise Cafe. He had a big pot he made soup in maybe ten inches in diameter and a foot high. Whenever we looked into it, there were always cockroaches floating on top of the soup. He would dish up some soup, pick out the cockroaches and serve it. I always wondered how many cockroaches he couldn't see, and the customers ate. At the Sunrise Cafe, you could buy a hamburger steak with potatoes, the whole meal for thirty-five cents! But it was hard to forget about the cockroaches when you ate there.

He also had a two-gallon can of cream. Because he didn't have any refrigeration, he left water running over the can to keep it cool. Sometimes when he hired us to wash dishes for him, we would pick up that can of cream and drink right from the can. He never caught us.

There used to be the Alaska Junk Store located where the Mission is now. The kids in town used to sell bottles to the Alaska Junk man there. He'd put them behind the building after he bought them, but the kids would go around back and steal the bottles and sell them back to him again. They did this over and over again until he caught them. Then he started keeping them inside. He also had a big junkyard on the corner of G and Astor where he had scrap metal. The kids used to crawl over the fence and get bicycle frames and make all kinds of toys for themselves. They'd put together a bicycle with real small wheels and then they would ride that down the street.

When we were kids we used to play *Kick the Can*. We'd get four or five guys together and one kid would kick the can and then he would run after the can and bring it back to the place he kicked it. While he was gone everybody would go hide and then he'd have to go find everyone. They'd hide under the house or behind the woodpile. If he couldn't find anybody, one of the guys would sneak out from his hiding place and kick the can while the other guy was out looking. Then the first guy would have to kick the can again. We had a lot of fun with this game.

There was a bakery a block away from where we played. They had hot pastry and we'd buy rubber necks right out of the oven. We'd eat those and play in the street. One time I told a kid to go down and get me a half pint of milk and I'd give him half of it. In those days the cream was on the top and that was the best part. So he came back, handed me the bottle, half empty and said, "I've already had my half." I got a bum deal out of that.

Dad gave us half the money we got from selling crabs, and we put it in a little oval bank. Whenever Dad left us boys alone during the summer while he went fishing and we wanted money, we went to our banks. We used a knife to pry the bottom and twist it a little bit and the dimes would come out. Then we'd twist it a little more and the nickels came rolling out. Then the quarters and then the half-dollars. One time my dad came back from fishing and said, "Well boys, let's get our banks and we'll go to the bank and deposit the money." My heart sank because I knew my bank was just about empty and so was my brother's. But we went to the bank and handed our little banks to the teller. She had the key and opened them. My brother had fifty cents left in his and I had about a dollar fifty in mine. We should have had about twenty dollars in each. On the way home I was sure we were going to get a licking so we walked about ten or fifteen feet ahead of our dad. All the way we were hoping there would be someone at the house, a visitor or something, so he wouldn't give us a spanking. He didn't, but that was the end of the banks.

One time my brother and I played hooky from school, but we were more afraid of Dad than anything else, and feared he was going to see us walking around downtown while he drove the truck around delivering crabs. It took all the fun out of it, so we didn't do it again.

When my brother and I were going to high school, we used to go to the dances at Birch Bay, a summer resort about twenty miles north of Bellingham. The fellow I went with made home brew. We were kind of shy and were afraid to go up and ask a girl to dance, so we'd take beer in the car and drink beer on the way to the dance. It made it easier to ask the girls. My brother used to steal wine from my dad. My dad made wine about every three months. He didn't drink water. He just drank wine. That was the custom in Croatia where he had come from. This was during the prohibition time, so he was afraid someone would squeal on us and he'd get pinched. Dad had moved the crab operation from the float shack to our home so it would be easier for us to get to school. But, because of his wine-making, Dad said we could only let one kid come in our house and no other kids were allowed. The only reason he let this one kid come and visit was because his mother was making beer, so he figured he wasn't about to squeal. When my dad wasn't home we let other kids come over, but when we heard Dad drive up, the kids ran out the back door.

Every Saturday night my brother would take a whiskey flask of my dad's wine. At first he diluted it with water so Dad wouldn't notice any was gone, but when my dad tasted it, he knew the wine wasn't the same. So he'd ask Jack if he had taken wine. Jack would deny it. Then he stopped diluting it but every Sunday Dad would miss the wine. Jack hid the flask out in the lumber pile, but my dad would find it. No matter where he hid it, Dad found it. He never missed. It seemed their minds ran in the same direction. Sunday morning Dad would find the flask with just a little left in it, and ask Jack if he had taken his wine. Jack denied it every week, but my dad would give him a beating. It happened over and over again. Jack figured it was worth it. During Prohibition, he couldn't get liquor anywhere else, so he figured it was worth the beating to get the wine.

One time we were at a dance with about four quarts of beer for the two of us. We'd go out at intermission and drink some beer and then go back to the dance. On this evening, we used up a couple of quarts and the rest was in the car. On the way home, I was just about two blocks from our house when a cop stopped me. I didn't know how long he had been following me, but I guess I was driving a little unsteady. He asked me to open up the back of the car. I knew we had some beer left back there and that we were in big trouble. But I had to do it. So I opened up the back and there wasn't any beer there. My brother had raided our car and took it all. Boy, was I ever glad he took it.

We'd go sometimes to dig clams for crab bait up at Blaine. We had a little boat and we'd go across to a little spit where there was a clam reserve owned by the Alaska Packers. They didn't allow anyone to dig clams there. But, almost every week we'd go out at night and use a gas light and dig three- to four-hundred pounds of clams. We'd sneak over there because it was fast digging and the clams were better than other places. Sometimes they'd come down and kick us out but then we'd go back. I guess they got used to us, as we were kind of steady customers for those clams. I think one of the reasons we did so well in the crab business was we used good bait.

My dad used to deliver crabmeat to all the restaurants in Bellingham. One time my dad was delivering about fifty pounds of it for a big convention at a hotel there. While he was waiting for the cook, somebody sent their steak back because it wasn't done enough. The Japanese cook got so mad, he took the steak, spit on it, threw it on the floor, stepped on it, put it back on the grill for a few minutes, and then he put it back on the plate and sent it back to the customer. The guy got his steak cooked a little more, but he didn't know what else was done to it.

CHAPTER 2
The Beginning of a Career

I started fishing out in the ocean on the boat *Elector* in 1929. I was sixteen. It was my dad's boat. He didn't know too much about fishing, since he had always been in the crab business, so he hired skippers to run the boat. It is important to have someone running the boat who knows what they are doing. There are a lot of snags in the Sound and a guy could lose a whole net if he got caught up in one. I've seen guys up on the dock working for two or three days to fix up nets that were snagged.

Most of the skippers he hired were Slavs from the Island of Vis, Yugoslavia. This is where my Dad was from also. It is a

Elector used for dragging and sharking out of Astoria, Oregon.

seventeen-mile-long island in the Adriatic. On one side of the island is the town of Kamisa. Most of the fishing took place out of Kamisa. They fished for sardines and there was a cannery there.

On the other side, near the town of Vis, they raised grapes. My dad's folks raised grapes in Vis. When World War I broke out and they began drafting young men into the armed forces, a lot of them left and came to the United States. Many tended to settle on the West Coast, in San Pedro, San Francisco, Seattle, Tacoma, Everett, Anacortes, and Bellingham. They had been fishermen in Yugoslavia, so a lot of them got jobs on the boats in the area. Many of them only spoke Slav.

In our home my mother was Irish and my dad was Slav. My dad spoke to my mother in English and we didn't learn to speak Slav in our home. The only Slav I learned was a few words I picked up from the guys on the boats. Naturally, we picked up most of the cuss words first. But I never really learned to speak it.

We fished the Salmon Banks off San Juan Island near the Lime Kiln light. We were really close to shore, right by the kelp off the rocks. It was so deep right off the rocks, you could get really close. This one skipper would sit on top of the pilothouse and steer with his feet. They didn't have flying bridges in those days. There was a little platform and the wheel was sticking out of the pilothouse from the inside. We would fish the tide in one place and then run half an hour or so to another spot.

Most of the time we fished off Point Roberts. It was a good place to fish because when the fish leave the San Juan Islands, they have to come up through Point Roberts to get to the Frazier River in Canada, so we had a pretty good crack at the fish there. They passed Salmon Banks first on their way to the spawning ground.

On a big ebbing low tide and a westerly wind, the fish would back down into US water. We called them blowbacks. We'd have a man up in the mast, and he would be able to see these big brown spots in a mass as the fish were in big schools. We'd go up there and lay the net out and go right around the fish. Sometimes you could almost load up a boat this way, there were so many fish.

We purse seined during the fall season for salmon outside of Tatoosh Island, off the extreme northwest corner of Washington state, at the entrance of the Strait of Juan de Fuca. In those days, we could see the fish fin in the water. They would be right on the surface. We would take the boat right around and come right back to the skiff, making a circle and pull the net in. Soon they outlawed this kind of fishing in the open sea because they couldn't count the run of salmon. That was a good idea because they needed to regulate the fishery.

We anchored every night off Neah Bay and then in the daytime we would fish salmon around the Swiftsure Lightship. This was before the breakwater was built so it was all open to the ocean. Although we anchored in the bay, big swells would come in.

I remember one of the first times I went out on the *Elector*. We were running from Neah Bay out to Cape Flattery to go fishing for silvers and we ran into some of those big swells. The boat was going up and down and I got seasick and I said, "Boy, this is not for me!" I hate getting seasick. I thought it was about the worst thing that could happen to a fellow. It is a miserable situation. But of course it was for me! I didn't know it then, but I was to spend my entire life on that ocean!

We were getting a few pennies for each fish, which, even in those days, was poor. We got a lot of fish in Bellingham Bay so we just came in and called the Salvation Army and let them have it. We couldn't make much money anyway so it was better to give them away. Boy, you ought to have seen the people come down to get that free fish. It didn't take long to get rid of it. We did that once in a while. People were in bad shape during the Depression and they really enjoyed getting something for nothing.

On the *Elector* we made raisin wine on the bow in thirty-gallon wooden barrels. We'd put the raisins in a big sack, tie the top, and drop it into the barrel. There was a spigot on the barrel. The crew would just hold their glasses under the spigot and fill them up. One day the boys ran out of wine. They told me to clean out the barrel so they could make another batch. I took the lid off the barrel and pulled out the sack, opened it up, and it was completely full of live maggots. And here these guys had been drinking this wine to the very last drop.

In 1929 Dad sent my brother down to Seattle to go to the YMCA school where they taught navigation. He was down there a couple of months. When he came back my dad said to him, "Okay, we're going to leave Bellingham for Cape Flattery. You figure out our course." So my brother was in the chart room trying to figure out what course to take. He came out and gave us the course. An oldtimer was running the boat. He had been out to the Cape many times and said, "That's funny! I never steered this course before. It doesn't seem right." My brother had the wrong course. He had been studying celestial navigation, which we really didn't need. My dad was disappointed. He had sent him down there to learn navigation and he couldn't even lay out a course to Cape Flattery.

꜡

When I graduated from high school in 1930, I went to Alaska on the boat *Leader*. The skipper was Antone Costello. He built a brand-new 58-foot Alaska Limit seiner. There was a law in those days that said you couldn't go to Alaska with anything bigger than a 50-foot keel, so this boat was the biggest they would allow in southeastern Alaska. We went from Bellingham up to the Inian Islands. They're not too far from Cape Spencer. We fished out of Dundas Bay. They had a cannery there at that time and they also had floating fish traps on the island there. In this place they couldn't have a stationary trap, driven into the bottom with pilings. Because of the ice flows and the strong tides, the only thing they could use was the floating trap.

We fished salmon in that area. There's a lot of tide running there, so it was hard to keep the net from getting fouled on itself. When we'd raise the net, it would be a big tangle between the purse rings. It was a great place to fish, but what a hassle it was too. But we did it.

I was skiff man. I handled the skiff that was used to pull the big net off the big boat. At that time there was no power in the skiffs. So the skiff was stationary and the big boat would lay the net out in a half circle, holding it open for about twenty minutes or so, allowing the fish to get into the net. Then the large boat would drop the net, and take the end of the towline to the skiff, laying out towline as he ran to the skiff. The skiff man then threw the line on his end of the net to the big boat. The seiner would then pull both ends of the net together. After the ends are together, the crew began pursing up the net like drawing the string on a Bull Durham sack.

To prevent the fish from escaping under the boat, we also used a plunger, usually a coffee can nailed to the end of a long pole. We would plunge this up and down in the water to create a white foam, which scared the fish away from the boat and back into the net. And that's how we fished.

When I look back on it, I see all the changes that took place in purse seining for salmon. Each change made fishing a lot easier.

At first they used a manila rope to purse the rings at the bottom of the net. These ropes wore out quickly. So we went from rope to cable.

Then we started putting power in the skiffs so we could tow both ends of the net at the same time. That sped up the operation and was more effective.

Later a Slav fellow invented the Puretic block, which took a lot of the work out of purse seining. It was way up on the top of the boom, powered by hydraulics. It was a V-type that took the cork line and everything else up to the top of the boom. It meant no one had to pull the net over the stern. The block did all the work. All we had to do was pile up the slack from the power block down on the boat. So we didn't need turntables anymore and it sure made it a lot easier. We also could have a smaller crew and save money.

Later they invented this big drum to pull the net in. This huge reel, as wide as the boat and six feet in diameter, wound the net right up.

All these changes made such a difference that I once heard of one man who ran a seine boat all by himself. He didn't even use a skiff, just a buoy that he would throw out. He would run around, come back to the buoy, and then close up. It didn't work that well, but he did it. Most of the boats had three or four men on a drum

Leader on my first salmon fishing to Alaska in 1930.

seine. That meant you could have a cook as well as a crew. You could make up to twelve sets in one day this way.

The drum seine was really a big invention for the salmon boats. However, drum seines were not allowed in Alaska. So, the boats up there just used the power block.

Well, my first summer on the *Leader* in Alaska was long and miserable. It rained a lot of the time. The skipper would get excited and lay out the net without paying much attention to where he laid it. He would see the fish jump and just go after them. But in his excitement he wasn't careful about where he was, and often he would lay out where there were rocks. He'd snag the bottom, tear the net all to pieces and the crew spent sometimes two or three days on the dock fixing the net. But, that's the way he was. When he'd see the fish, he just couldn't wait and he'd start yelling for us to let her go. And we might be over a reef or the rocks and the nets would be a mess again. So, it was a pretty long, miserable summer. But each member of the eight-man crew made a thousand fifty bucks that season, which was pretty good money in those days. This was during the Depression.

In 1931, my dad built a brand new Alaska Limit seiner. Because he enjoyed the Island there on his way to America, he decided to name his first new boat the *New Zealand*. It was built in Seattle by the Barbee Ship Building Company. They built about five boats at the same time, all the same size. One was the *Governor Hartley*, one was the *Progress*, one was the *Rio Grande*, another the *Rio Janeiro*, and we were building the *New Zealand*.

I was working in the shipyard in those days while our boat was being built. When they were ready to launch the *Governor Hartley*, they had a big party. It was on a Saturday night. They had speeches and a lot of special things. On Monday morning, I went down to the restaurant to get my breakfast. We always went to this same restaurant.

The waitress said, "Where are you going?"

I said, "I'm going to work."

She said, "No, you're not going to work."

I said, "What do you mean, 'I'm not going to work'?"

She said, "Well, Saturday night they had a big fire in the shipyard and it burnt up. They had a big paint fight, and the guys were throwing paint at each other and they got drunk and they had a big mess and then the yard caught on fire."

So, I didn't go to work. The boat my dad was having built didn't burn as it had already been launched. This was the first boat he ran himself.

When the *New Zealand* was being built, I went to navigation school in the same place my brother had gone. I did this to prepare myself to be the navigator to take the boat to Alaska. I got my license for a 65-foot boat to take passengers for hire. I studied *Hanson's Handbook,* which had the courses all laid out. It showed topographical details about the land. It also told about each of the lights and showed pictures of them, and gave an elapsed time between various points. So, as long as you checked your tides and time, even in the fog, you'd get to the right place at the right time.

After the boat was finished and after the new 3-cylinder, 75-horsepower Atlas diesel was installed, the factory man made the trip from Seattle to Bellingham to show me how to run the new engine.

We had a choice of the traditional valves in the head or what they called cage valves. We chose the cage valves so you could grind the valves without taking the head off the engine.

The technician from the factory told me I would have to watch the fuel pump and water pumps. Since this engine had salt-water cooling, you had to make sure the water pumps were working as well as the fuel pumps. Fuel was pumped from the main tank to the fifteen-gallon day tank. If the engine stopped, you had to first make sure the day tank was filled with fuel. Then you had to take the air out of all the fuel lines and get solid fuel back into the lines with thirty-eight hundred pounds of fuel pressure before you could get it started again. This would take thirty minutes or so. Then you had to have three hundred pounds of air pressure to start the engine again. So, it was a complicated process.

The man from the factory said I wouldn't have any trouble as long as I watched these things, and he was right. This was a good, trouble-free engine and became the most popular engine on the West Coast.

After we took our first trip salmon fishing, we went back to Bellingham and lived on the boat. We slept in the stateroom right behind the pilothouse. My dad slept in the upper bunk and I took the lower. I'd go chasing around at night, but I didn't want the old man to know what time I came in. Now he always snored. So every time he would snore, I'd take a step from the door closer to my bunk. When I finally got to the bunk, I had to do the same thing getting into bed. The mattress made a noise, so I kind of eased myself into it, one snore at a time. It took me a long time to get in. But if I rushed it and made a noise in between snores, he would wake up every time, turn on the light and check his watch.

In 1932, we took a load of produce to southeast Alaska. A produce man went along. We were going to split the profit after expenses. We had four hundred boxes of apples, many sacks of potatoes and bananas, and just about everything you could think of. We stopped in a little Alaskan village and found out another boat with produce had already been there a week before us and the natives were well supplied with all the produce they could use. We stopped

New Zealand with a load of sockeye almon at Bristol Bay in 1934.

in Wrangell, Alaska, put up notices and posters all over town but didn't sell hardly a thing. Then we went to Petersburg and then to Ketchikan and tried selling both places, but there wasn't much luck. We ended up consigning the whole load to a guy in Ketchikan, but he never paid us a dime. So, the trip was a bust and we headed back to Bellingham.

I remember heading south. It was snowing and freezing. We had no fathometer or radio. The steering rods ran through a one-inch pipe along each side of the deck. My father was steering and he was a good helmsman, but he didn't move the wheel much. It was so cold the steering rods froze in the pipe. We had to take a blowtorch to thaw them out. Then Dad kept moving the wheel so they wouldn't freeze. We also hit a lot of logs on the way. Although we didn't do any damage to the boat, it was quite a trip.

The next year we went to southeastern Alaska and fished again around the Inian Islands, the same place we had fished the year before. The fishing wasn't too good that year, so we didn't make much money. So we went back to Puget Sound. When the season opened, we fished around Point Roberts. They had lots of fish traps in those days between Point Roberts and Blaine. Boundary Bay was just full of them. Each company owned their own sites and placed their traps there.

These fishing traps were made of pilings driven into the bottom, a whole line of them, maybe as much as a block long. In between the pilings was a wire mesh. They used the wire to lead the salmon into the fish trap. Each trap had a shack on it with a watchman. People would come and try to rob the traps. When the fish were in the water, they didn't belong to anybody, so there was a lot of trouble with trap robbers. There were times a watchman would sell a load of salmon to the fish pirates. So, the fish trap owners put on patrol boats to stop this kind of business. There was one guy who was so mistrusted, they offered him $250 a month to just sit in front of the cannery office, so they'd know he wasn't out pirating their traps. Then they finally outlawed the traps and then everything was purse seining and gillnetting from then on. The Indian tribes were using reef nets.

In 1934, we took a charter as a salmon tender in Bristol Bay, Alaska. I remember going across the gulf there. The skipper was a Norwegian fellow named Art Nelson. We left Cape Spencer and took a course straight to the Shumagins, and from there we went up through False Pass and into the Bering Sea. Going through False Pass, I could see the boat ahead of us. The water was all murky because the boat in front of us was hitting bottom as he went through. The channels were poorly marked in those days, so it was a frightening trip.

I remember when we got to the Bering Sea, out in the open, as far as the eye could see, there were these small 30-foot open crab boats. They were fishing King Crab with tangle nets. And then in the distance you'd see a great big mother ship. I guess they probably pulled these small boats up at night. There were about seven or eight guys in these boats, and we stopped at one of them and tried to bum some fish to cook, but they wouldn't give us any. They didn't understand us, I think. And we didn't understand their language, so we didn't get any fish. So we went on to the Nushagak River where we were tendering for the *Santa Flavia*, a sailing ship nearly three hundred feet long, converted to a fish cannery.

A *tender* is a large boat that goes out and picks up the fish from the gillnet boats and brings the salmon to the cannery. Every year there were boats that were lost. A storm would come up and they had too many fish on board, and they'd go down. They didn't have any power so they were helpless in the storms. A fellow by the name of Bradford owned the cannery and his wife owned the Lowe Trading Post in Dillingham.

We went into the trading post there which had a big stove. Sitting there were some Indian squaws. They must have weighed about 200 or 250 pounds, maybe more. But the real attraction was this other woman who was holding a big stack of silver dollars. She would drop them, one at a time, from one hand to another. She was trying to get the native women excited by the sight of those silver dollars. She wanted to buy their fox furs. This was the first time I had ever seen bargaining like this.

I met a fellow there who manned dog sleds for the trading posts. He did trapping too. He told me the Nushagak River froze over in the wintertime. That's when they'd go trapping for fox furs. He had a copper chain around his wrist. It was really a crude looking thing. I said, "What are you wearing that thing for?" He said, "Oh, I'll tell you. I almost died here with rheumatism or arthritis, whichever it was, and an Indian made me this copper chain and I put it on and wore it. In about six months it turned black, and then it started to shine again. When the chain started to shine, I lost my rheumatism and I'm never going to take this off. I'll leave it on until I die."

We never went back to that trading post, so I don't know what happened to him, but now I wear a copper chain. And I don't know whether it works or not. But I don't have any rheumatism, so I'm not taking mine off until I die either.

We towed sailboats from the Nushagak River to Egegik, which is about forty to fifty miles away. We had to get them to the fishing grounds for the beginning of the season. We towed about six boats at a time. No boat with a motor was allowed to fish in Bristol Bay. We had power, but we were a tender. So, we towed the boats wherever they wanted to go. Then we went from boat to boat to pick up their fish at the end of each day and bring them back to the cannery.

One night the cannery operator dumped ten thousand fish. They just threw away ten thousand sockeyes that night. They were getting old and they didn't dare can them, so they had to dump them. There was always new fish coming.

Fish buying power scows anchored out in the bay where they bought the fish. I was going out in a skiff to one of these scows. I was rowing along and, by golly, you could feel the fish hit the oars–the fish were that thick in the water. That was where the Naknek and the Kuichak Rivers joined.

The son of the Superintendent of the cannery was working on one of the power scows. He hung a piece of gillnet in the river where the barges were anchored and, just hanging there off the barge, he caught a lot of fish. He made enough money with this little piece of gillnet to pay for his schooling. I think he only got ten cents a piece for those fish. That's how good the fishing was.

↩

While we were tendering up there in Bristol Bay, the skipper hired a cook out of Seattle. He was a baker. He took a quarter of a beef and hung it up in the rigging. It was kind of cool in Alaska so we just hung this meat up there. Then we'd just cut off what we needed and we'd have fresh meat. We also had live chickens on the boat. I think a lot of the seiners did that.

The skipper asked the guy, "You're a baker, but we never see anything come out of the oven. How is that?" "Oh," the cook said, "I bake with machinery. I don't bake anything small like that." So he was a big time bakery operator. When we got up to Bristol Bay, we started getting some fresh meat from the cannery there, so we didn't cut any more off this quarter of beef that hung in the rigging. But then, after a couple of weeks the cannery cut us off and didn't give us any more. So the cook went up and cut a chunk off that quarter of beef and brought it down to the galley to fix dinner.

I was the engineer on that boat. I had just come up out of the engine room and there was this awful smell. I asked the cook, "What smells? Man! There's something rotten!" He had this cut of beef spread out there on the table, all ready to cook. I bent over and smelled it. That was it! I said, "Hey, this meat is rotten!" But he wouldn't believe me, so I told him, "Well, I'm not eating any of that meat, I'll tell you that. You can eat it if you want, but I'm not!" He wrapped it all up and took it away. He asked some of the others on the ship whether they thought it was any good or not. I guess then he threw it away. At least, he didn't serve it for dinner.

≈

The engine on our boat was a 3-cylinder, 75-horsepower Atlas Diesel. Every time you'd stop it, it wouldn't start again. You would have to move the flywheel back to a certain mark in order to start it with air. Normally, you'd pull the flywheel forward, but you had to go almost twice as far around to get to the mark. By pushing it backward, it was a lot quicker. So I always pushed the flywheel backward. Now there was a bar about one and three-eighths inches in diameter and three feet long that we used to move the flywheel. One time I forgot to take the bar out. I gave it the air and, man, oh man! You ought to have heard it. It broke all the floorboards in the engine room. All the guys came down to see what was going on. Man, I thought maybe it even knocked the planking out of the bottom of the boat. But, it didn't do any damage to our planking on the outside. But it sure broke the floor up, and it bent that bar so bad we couldn't use it. I had to heat it up to get it straight. Boy, it sure scared me. But anyway, that's one of the things that happens. A fellow makes a mistake, and that's the way it is.

One year we went fishing to the Shumagin Islands with the New Zealand. We had a cook called the economical cook. Oh, he was a good cook. He made donuts. Boy, boats would tie up along side of us, and everybody wanted to go in and bum some of that nice fresh pastry he made. He made a big pot of applesauce. He put it on the table, and we gobbled up half of it, but he made so much we couldn't eat it all. So, he put it in a drawer in the galley and let it sit there about three or four days. It began to mold. We happened to look in there and saw the applesauce had a little fuzz on the top of it. Then he made a deep sea apple pie, and we all knew he used the applesauce for the pie. So, he put the fresh pie on the table but nobody touched it because we knew the applesauce was in there. He didn't say a thing, but he took the applesauce out of the pie and made a steamed pudding with a nice lemon sauce over it. And boy! Was it ever good! The guys really gobbled it up. He had made quite a bit and we didn't eat one of those puddings, so he put that in the drawer. Then he told the guys, "You didn't eat all the applesauce, and you didn't eat the apple pie, but you ate those apples after all. They were in the steamed pudding!" And that's why I called him the economical cook. But, you know, we had to throw that other steamed pudding out. Nobody wanted to touch it.

⏝

After the salmon charter to Bristol Bay, I went back to Puget Sound and got a job carrying the mail and freight for the Waters Brothers. I took the mail from Bellingham to Point Roberts. You can only get to Point Roberts one of two ways. You can drive through Canada, through customs and then out to the little piece of land that juts out below the United States/Canadian border or you go by boat. Usually the 65-foot *Tulip* made the mail run each day. When it went on dry dock for repairs, we took over. There wasn't much work for the salmon boats during the winter months except for dragging for bottom fish. Most of the skippers had to pull their boats out of the water for the winter, so we were pleased to have some work.

Sometimes we fished on the south side of Lummi Island. Occasionally we ran into Bellingham when the tide wasn't right for fishing. One day we started talking to another boat about going to town to have some fun. We were just kidding because we were really going to Elisa Island to tie up to one of the piling there. One of our crew members had heard us talking to this other boat and he went below and shaved, put on his good clothes, and after we shut down the engines and tied up to the piling, it was dark and this guy came up on deck only to find we weren't in Bellingham at all. He was furious, but we had a good laugh over it.

⏝

My dad used to run the boat to Point Roberts for salmon. He was the sort of guy who didn't like competition. A lot of the boats were taking turns at the light at Point Roberts. On the ebb tide you'd wait about twenty minutes for one boat to lay out their net, and then he'd drift out of the way and the next boat could lay out. I told my dad, "Why don't you go over there and get in position and get a chance to get some of those fish? Those guys are doing good." But he didn't like the competition. He'd go on the outside of the guys. His net wasn't deep enough so he never caught much. So, I used to argue with him a lot and he'd kick me off the pilothouse.

I always insisted, "You'd better go over there with the rest of the guys or you're not going to make anything." But he wouldn't listen to me. So, finally he let me run the boat. When I was running the boat, I'd go fish where I thought we needed to be. In order to catch fish, there's a lot of dog eat dog. Everybody's out to cork you. Two boats see the same fish jump. One skipper starts to lay out his net and the other guy lays out about the same time, except he's in front of you. Since the guy in the second spot wouldn't catch a thing, he has to stop and pull his net in. There's no use laying your net outside of him.

The boat *Avalon*, owned by a guy by the name of Evich, was always corking us. I don't know how many times he corked us. We'd see the fish, get in position and he'd lay out right in front of us. And, oh man, it would make me so darned mad. Anyway, that's the way it was. It was dog eat dog. The fish have to be almost in your net before you can lay out, because if you lay out too much ahead of the fish, another boat will set out in front of you. There was a lot of that going on. But, that's the way it was.

In the days I started running the boat there wasn't much money to be made. There were no big seasons and we had Sunday laws, which meant you couldn't legally fish on Sundays. There was no big money to be made in fishing, but you could make a living at it.

Before we started dragging in Bellingham Bay, we got a job with the Indians catching and selling herring by the barrel to the Alaska halibut boats. They stopped in Hales Pass, a channel between Lummi Island and the mainland. The Indians caught the herring and kept them alive in net ponds until they were sold. We were happy for the work because it gave us and the boat something to do in the off-season.

George with his Durant in 1936.

CHAPTER 3
A Life on My Own

In 1936, I decided to leave home. I had a Durant car. It was a four-door, and Paul Glenovich and Nick Sirkovich and I took off for California in the Durant. Dad had two brothers and a sister in San Pedro, so we had a place to stay while we were job hunting. We were going down there to see if we could get a start in the sardine and tuna fishery there. The sardine season begins in San Francisco and then the fish move south, so the season ends in the San Pedro area. On the way down to San Francisco, we went by the Flyshacker Zoo by San Francisco. We didn't have very good brakes on this car, and some people were crossing the street. There was a policeman there and he blew his whistle at me to stop because the people had already started to go across. I couldn't stop, so I had to turn quickly, and I almost ran over him. I finally stopped about a hundred feet past him. He came over and said, "Hey, what's the matter with you?!" I said, "Well," (I had to make up a story quickly.) "I, I, I don't know. I just got excited, I guess." I didn't dare tell him we didn't have any brakes or we would have been stuck right there. But he didn't give us a ticket, so off we went on our way to San Pedro.

The Italians were the first ones in the sardine business in Monterey. The crew members of those first boats were making good money and driving big fancy cars. The Italians and the Japanese were in competition to get the largest boats in Washington state. In those days a 70-foot boat was big. As many as ten partners would get together and build a new boat.

I got a job as engineer on a sardine boat, the *Hawk II*. Andrew Xitco was the skipper. It had a 5-cylinder, 200-horsepower Atlas Imperial diesel, the same kind we had in the *New Zealand*. This was a 78-foot boat that held 100 tons of sardines.

～

We were fishing for a floating processor vessel named the *Lansing*. It was anchored just north of the Golden Gate. It had two big booms on each side of the ship so two boats could unload at the same time. There was a big hopper they lowered down on the boat and then a large hose sucked up the fish from the boat into the processor. We had to brail them out of the hold and put them in the hopper. The nice thing about the floating processor was that we could make two trips in one night. A lot of boats fished for processing plants on shore, and they could only make one trip a day because they had to run in to San Francisco.

We fished nights in the dark of the moon. You can't fish in the daytime because you can't see the fish. When you run at night and go over a school of sardines, the phosphorus in the water lights up. It's just like throwing milk in the water, and you can tell how many sardines are underneath the boat. Sometimes you could say, "Oh, there's 35 ton there, or there's 20 ton or 50 ton, or even 100 ton." Then we went around them and laid out the net on them and we'd get almost what we saw. It was pretty easy to judge. We got ten dollars a ton for sardines. So that's what we did.

～

Around San Francisco we were fishing for sardines, but we would get a lot of anchovies in the net. Both are little fish, but we were after sardines. The anchovies get their heads gilled in the one-and-a-half-inch mesh. When we lifted up a net with the boom and it was filled with anchovies, it just glittered. We called it a Christmas tree. One time we got tons of anchovies instead of sardines and had to go into San Francisco, pull the net out on the dock, lift the net to the top of the boom and, with scoop shovels broke the heads off the fish so they fell out of the net.

One guy had a great idea. He used the steam hose from the sardine plant, sprayed hot water on the big pile of net, and cooked the anchovies right there in the net. Then he went out and made a set with the net and all the cooked fish just fell out. The net was clean enough to go fishing again. Pretty soon we were able to tell where to fish for sardines and where there were only anchovies. We just wouldn't set the net when it looked like anchovies.

I'll never forget the time we were tied up at San Francisco on one of the docks by Fisherman's Wharf. There was an automobile tire right in back of the boat. It was floating upright. There was about five to six inches of tire above the surface and the rest was below the water. We backed into that thing, and I told the skipper, "Gee, there was a tire back there and now it's gone." Then I heard some noise down in the engine room. The tire must have gotten into the wheel, judging by the noise it made. He tried to get it loose. He'd go forward and backward with the controls on the engine. This engine didn't have a reverse gear. The engine ran two ways. If you wanted to back up, you had to reverse the engine. The cam shaft would slide, so you'd give it air and it would start either way. So he tried to get rid of the tire, but couldn't. So he said, "Ah, we're going to go out fishing anyway." So we went out down around Pigeon Point, which is around twenty to thirty miles below the San Francisco lightship, and we made a set there and, by golly, we got a full load of sardines. When we started to go back to Frisco to deliver to the processor, nothing happened! The skipper put it in gear, and he hollered to me and said, "Hey Musky! What's going on down there?" (My nickname is Musky.) I went down to the engine room, and I came back and told him, "The engine's running, the shaft's turning. Our troubles are either under the fish or we lost the wheel or something." So we got towed in, put her on dry dock, and sure enough, the propeller was gone. The big brass nut that holds the propeller on had come off and there wasn't a scratch in the threads but the propeller was gone. It must have been the tire. So we had to go buy another wheel to get back in business.

⌣

John Blum, the captain of the *Albatross*, came over to ask if I could help him with some engine problems. He told me he had a Superior. I had never heard of that engine. He thought it needed to be over-hauled, but he couldn't afford to do that, so he told me where the oil pumps were. There was a sixteen-inch inspection plate on the side of that area of the engine. We took the plate off and I told him to start the engine. I could see a loose three-quarter-inch union where oil was just flowing out. I tightened the union and it worked just fine. He called me the "best engineer." I told him I was just a curious person. I like to see how things work.

After the sardines, they went for tuna in Mexico, so I changed boats. A friend of mine, Mitchell Kuljis, built a new 85-foot sardine boat in 1937 named the *Kingfisher*. Because I was friends with Mitchell's son Andy, I got a job on this boat and fished one sardine season.

One night we didn't get any sardines. The skipper told Andy to take the boat in to San Francisco while he got some sleep. On the way, Andy saw a school of sardines flipping on the surface, so, even though he wasn't the skipper, he made a set and got a full load of sardines. When he was pursing up, the boat shook and woke the skipper. He didn't know what was happening. He was mad and glad at the same time: mad that a crew member made a set and glad that he got a full load.

While aboard the *Kingfisher* we made a trip for tuna in Mexico. We got four hundred blocks of crushed ice. There was no refrigeration at that time, so we had to have a lot of ice. I remember the cook had a big canvas bag of chickens. The bag must have been about two feet in diameter, so he had a lot of chickens in there. He kept the chicken bag buried in the ice. We'd take out enough for three or four days at a time, because every time we opened the hatch, the ice would melt. It would go down six to twelve inches. So we didn't want to open the fish hold very often. After about two weeks, we took this bag of chickens out, and, by golly, all the chickens on the outside of the bag were good, but all the chickens in the middle of the bag were rotten. So we lost at least half of them.

↜

We made one set down off Cabo San Lucas and got about 47 ton of tuna. Then we took off for home. I don't know why we went home because the boat could hold over a hundred ton, but the skipper wanted to go so we went up to San Pedro to deliver. We didn't make any money because the profit was in the 50-plus ton we *didn't* catch. It was a bum deal for the crew.

↜

When we fished in Mexico we'd run, run, run full speed all day long in the hot sun and I could hardly stay awake. I can understand why the Mexicans take a siesta in the afternoon. When it's hot, it's really easy to go to sleep. I just can't stand the heat. I can't keep my eyes open. So I didn't like tuna fishing there very well.

꙰

The next boat I fished on was the *Farallon*. My cousin was running it. We were fishing out of San Francisco for sardines. We did fairly well. When the season was over we ran to San Pedro. We had a real San Francisco chef as a cook, and we sure had good eats. Storm warnings went up and the chef didn't like rough weather so he quit, and we had to leave the dock without a cook. It was a rough trip to Pedro, both because of the weather and no cook. But when we got to Pedro, standing on the dock was our old chef. We hired him back to fish the balance of the season.

꙰

The next year I got on another boat that was also fishing sardines. It was a big boat named the *St. Mary*, a 90-footer, and my cousin was running it. He got sick, and said, "Hey Musky, do you want to take the boat out?" I said, "Sure, why not. I'll take it." Well, when the crew heard that I was going to run the boat, they didn't want to go. They said, "What do you know about fishing?" "Well," I said, "I can run the boat. You guys can tell me how much fish there is there, and how to set the net. You guys do what you always do. The only difference is, I'm handling the boat. Anybody can handle a boat. Let's go and see what we can do."

So finally they agreed to go, and we went out and made two sets, and, by golly, we got 80 tons of fish, and a lot of boats missed out that night, so I felt pretty good. The first time running a boat that big and to catch 80 ton! That was pretty nice. The skipper was real happy because he was sick and couldn't have gone, and it gave me a chance to use some of my knowledge about sardine fishing.

꙰

In 1937, my dad had the *New Zealand* in San Pedro. He was down there getting into the sardine business too. He had a fellow running the boat by the name of Luka Padovan, and he had a son by the name of John. I had come back to fish with my dad. My dad said this John got into a fight every night. I said, "How could you do that?" So I thought I would go to town with him to see what happens. It was about nine or ten at night. There was a guy standing in one of these empty store buildings. John went up to the guy and he bumped him, for no reason. The guy said, "What's the big idea?" But this guy wasn't looking for a fight, so John went into beer joints and did the same thing. And that was how he got into a fight every night. I told him, "Boy, you could get your teeth broken or your nose busted like that. That's a poor deal." But he seemed to come out pretty good because he handled his dukes so well. He looked real young, but he was old enough to handle himself. But I didn't go up town with him anymore. I wasn't really a fighter.

We used to go down underneath the street in San Pedro and spend a lot of time at a gambling joint. They had some gambling ships outside of Long Beach all lit up like a Christmas tree, and they had little run-abouts to take you out there. It only cost about a dollar to go out and it was free to come back, because they knew you were going to come back broke anyway. The name of the gambling ship was the *Monte Carlo*, and it was anchored three miles off the coast so it would be legal. They did a pretty good business. There was another ship like it, and a lot of people from Los Angeles would go out there and gamble. We went out there one night because we had heard some guy won forty thousand bucks. They had gambling to fit anybody's pocket book, you know. It was really fun to see all this, because I had never seen it before.

There was an area in San Pedro we called *The Barbary Coast*. There was *Shanghi Reds, Bank Cafe,* and the *Alaska Inn*. There was a red light district too. It was really a wild place. There were a lot of fights and some of the guys would get the hell kicked out of them. Some of these guys were so beaten up we called them the *Walking Dead*. Their eyes were nearly swollen shut and they were all bloody.

The *New Zealand* was fishing mackerel down there. Before we left, we had a chance to charter the boat out to a Jewish fellow by the name of Max Gorby. He owned the California Marine Curing Packing Company. He wanted to charter the boat for six months, which was the whole season. We wanted $4,500 and he wanted to pay only $3,500. We couldn't agree on a price, so we were arguing. He had a little plywood shack where he did all his business. We were arguing in there, my father and I, and finally Gorby's wife came in. She sat down and listened for a while and then said, "What's the matter, you pip-puls. You wanta this much, and you wanta pay that much. What's the matter you don't spleet." So we split the difference and, by golly, we made a deal and he chartered the boat. But we didn't get our money from him. He couldn't make it fishing. Somehow there was not much fish that year. We had to get an attorney and get after him. We took a settlement for less money and got it squared away.

After we got the boat back from Gorby, we took the *New Zealand* back to Bellingham. I had an Auburn car I had bought down in California. It was a nice, fancy yellow sports car with a soft top. I had to go up with the boat and I couldn't drive the car at the same time, so we put the car across the deck, over the hatch and lashed her down and took off for Bellingham. When we came to Gray's Harbor, she started to blow northwest and it got really nasty, so we had to go in and get out of the weather. I thought we were going to lose that car overboard, it rolled so bad going across the bar there at Westport. But finally we got in. While we were there, President Roosevelt was just passing through. He had come to see them build the Liberty ships in Portland. It was a big deal because they built

Auburn taken from San Pedro to Bellingham on the deck of the *New Zealand* in 1938.

these ships really fast, in about ten days. I guess he came to the West Coast to see that, and he stopped in Hoquiam. We were only a block from him. They had secret police all over.

↜

Then the weather improved so we went on to Bellingham and unloaded the *Auburn*, and I used the car around town. I really enjoyed having it because it was a nice looking outfit. I used all the money I had from working in California to buy that car. If I hadn't bought the car I would have gambled with it, so I was really pleased to have the car.

↜

In 1939, we got our crab pots ready and went to Astoria with the *New Zealand* to look into the crab business. They were paying a dollar a dozen for crabs at first, but when they chopped the price to fifty cents a dozen, we quit.

We shopped around to see if we could sell some drag fish because we also had our drag nets with us. But nobody wanted to buy bottom fish. We were the only ones with dragging gear in Astoria, so the packers didn't handle it. We went to the Northwestern Ice and Cold Storage and they told us about Dr. McClean, a mink grower, who was secretary of the Mink Growers' Association. They used a lot of fish to feed their mink, although they would not pay much for it. I went up to see him, and he said, "Yeah, we'd use a lot of fish but we can only pay one and three-quarters cents a pound." I said, "That isn't very much for fish, but since we got the gear here, we'll try it."

So we went out and made a drag between buoy two and the lightship, and gee, we got all kinds of Dover (sole). We had all this fish, but the mink farmers didn't want to buy Dover. It was kind of slimy and they were afraid it would kill the mink. We had to throw it all back.

Art Anderson from the Columbia River Salmon Company helped me to get started by selling fish from his company. I unloaded at his dock, put the fish in boxes that were easy to unload to the mink farmers and we sold petrale, English, rex sole, flounder, and rock cod. That's how we got started in Astoria.

⌒

In winter 1939 the New England Fish Company said, "Bring some of that fish here. We want to try some of that." So I said, "Okay, we'll bring some, but I can't sell them for one and three-quarters cents a pound. I have to get at least three cents." They agreed to that. At first, we didn't take any ice when we went dragging. We went out about four in the morning and came back around seven or eight in the evening to unload. Then we'd go out again the next day if the weather was good.

In the beginning, the New England Fish Company didn't even want to send a guy down to take the fish off the boat. We had to unload with our own boom right on their dock in front of the doors and pile it up there, and then they'd come down and weigh them and let us know what we had. Then the next night we'd be right back in there with more fish.

That's the way we got them started taking bottom fish. Then in 1941 the war came on, and then there were lots of boats that came and started dragging.

⌒

A pilot boat guides the ships in and out of the Columbia River. When any ship comes into the river, they have to have a bar pilot on board for their insurance to be valid. So, they have to hire a pilot to take them over the bar and then another river pilot to take them up the river to Portland. Bar pilots from Astoria go out to sea to meet the ships. Lots of times they sent a pilot out on one ship and their ride back in on an incoming ship hadn't come yet. The pilots knew we were going in every night, so they'd come over to see me and say, "How about taking a pilot in?" Sure, we'd take him in. So, we'd let the pilot steer our boat and we would sort the fish out and clean up the boat on the way in. That way we could get a lot of work done. We took many pilots in, otherwise they would have to wait hours before the ship arrived, and they were always anxious to get home. It worked out well for both of us.

Things were rough just after the Depression. I think it was around Christmas. We were fishing on the *New Zealand*. We wanted to make ten bucks for Christmas. Just ten bucks! We went out and made a drag but didn't get much. It got dark and we anchored up for the evening off North Head Light, just north of the Columbia in about twenty fathom. And, by golly, I went to sleep and about five in the morning the boat started rolling and threw me out of the bunk. We were in the breakers. I had the engine spotted so we could give it the air and be all ready to go. It was blowing a westerly wind. The anchor line had broken and we were almost on the beach, so we headed out to the northwest and got out of there quick. We took a breaker getting out, but it didn't do any damage, so we got out okay.

We still wanted to make ten bucks, so we put the net out. There was a big swell. We had to have the wheel hard over to keep our depth, and we were still losing ground because the river was running out. And, by golly, it was such a big swell, the stanchion that held the trawl block was knocked down. It just took the lag bolts right out of the deck, fell down, and the block went right through a brand-new inch-and-three-quarter deck, between the beams. It hit so hard it broke the deck. It was a good thing we weren't back there because it would have killed us. So, now we couldn't make the ten bucks, no way! We had to go in because now we had lost the stanchion, and there was no way to re-hang the block.

In those days, we didn't have any winches on the *New Zealand*. We had rope gear, wooden doors, but we had no radio, dandelion, or fathometer. We had a wire up in the bow with a lead on it. We threw the lead overboard and then wound it up by hand. It was marked every fathom so we could determine the depth. We didn't have any winches to pull cable on. In fact, we didn't have any cable. We used ropes that were really old purse lines from Puget Sound, spliced together. We let the doors out with this rope. We put three or four turns on the gypsy head when we wanted to pull the doors in, and we'd have to back up (we had about twenty-five fathom between the doors and the net), full speed and get enough slack and then run up and put the lines on the gypsy head and pull the net in. Lots of times there'd be so much fish in the net, we had to take the doors all the way to the top of the boom to get a chance to get the lines on the gypsy head. We had no splitting straps in those days. We had the net laced up, and we'd have to open the bag and

Treo with a load of dogfish, 1940.

use a brailler about three feet in diameter with an eight-foot pole on it. You could pick up about three- to four-hundred pounds of fish at one time. We'd just push the brailler down into the fish and put a couple turns on the gypsy head, pick it up, swing it over, and dump it on the deck. That's the way we got fish out of the cod end of the net onto the boat.

In 1942, there was a fellow by the name of Barney Collinson who was running the *Matekla* for the Northwestern Ice and Cold Storage. They owned the boat and had ordered some drag gear from the East, and got everything so they could fish the way they did back there. They had a splitting strap, a cable going around the end of the cod end, which lets you meter how much you have to lift in relationship to whatever your boom can lift. So, if your boom can lift a ton, the splitting strap can cut her off at a ton. If you want more or less weight, you just put the splitting strap or the cable a little further up or down. In that way you can gauge it to whatever you want to lift with your boom without wrecking anything. We didn't know anything about a splitting strap until then.

⌒

Eventually we put on a splitting strap, steel cable, and power winches, which was a much better system, but when we first started we had some pretty tough times. We had to take a line out on the Olney Road and mark it every twenty-five fathom. We let the doors and net out, put a couple turns around the gypsy and slacked it off three to one for the depth we were in. We had a big coil of line on the deck and let it out to the depth we wanted. Then we started dragging. It was a tough way to do it, but we didn't have money for anything better, so that's the way we had to do it. But it got us started.

I bought used salmon webbing from Mr. Barbey who owned the Barbey Packing Company. They bought new webbing each time. The used web was plenty good for making dragnets for bottom fishing. I got it for twenty cents a pound and that saved me a lot of money.

CHAPTER 4

The First of Many

During 1940, Dad took the *New Zealand* back to Bellingham to fish salmon. It wasn't very profitable in Astoria. That was when I bought my first boat, the *Treo*. That was the boat that sank in the Columbia where we almost died.

After it was gone, I took off for California. A friend of mine was running the *Western Star,* so I got a job on her to go to Mexico for tuna. We were down there a month. Some Italians came with the boat and they sure didn't like tuna fishing. They couldn't stand it. They kept bellyaching all the time, saying, "What are we doing down here? Why did we come?" It was disgusting to the rest of us, but actually I didn't like fishing for tuna down there either. I wasn't used to hot weather. It doesn't agree with me!

We didn't make any money on this tuna trip, so I went back to Astoria and talked to Emil Urell about running his boat, the *Warren H.* He was a mink farmer. I then went down to San Francisco on the *Sunlight* to fish sardines again, and told him he could contact me there if he wanted me to run his boat. Sure enough! When I got to San Francisco there was a telegram from Urell, telling me we had a deal.

We were fishing for dogfish around the river at that time. Art Anderson, owner of the Columbia River Salmon Company, who had helped me sell my bottom fish to the mink farmers, then asked me to run the *Muzon* for him. That was when I got my draft papers. So I went to Bellingham to say good-bye to my dad. While I was there I went out to the Cat's Eye, a beer parlor on Marine Drive where a lot of fishermen hung out. I asked them why they weren't being drafted, and they told me that fishermen had deferments. I called Art Anderson and he told me to go to the draft board office in Bellingham and get a letter from them about their policy

The Tordensjold caught $44,000 of shark in one trip of the Oregon Coast.

on deferments for fishermen. It all worked out. I was deferred and went back to Astoria to run the *Muzon*.

In 1942, I went to Bellingham and went into partnership with my dad on the *Elector*. It was a lot better to own a boat than to be a "boat puller" on someone else's boat. My dad always told me it was better to work for yourself even if you made less money. This was a gas boat. It had winches and we rigged it up and put a bait tank on it so we could go tuna fishing. My brother Jack joined me. He is a year older than I am. We had a little gas engine to pump circulation water through the tank to keep the tuna bait alive. I had just gone up to the store to get something. Jack was working on the boat. He moved a gas line and hit the battery terminal and the darn boat blew up. Man, it blew the hatch covers right off the deck. I was coming back from the store and my brother was running off the boat, not looking back. His hair was all singed. He was yelling, "She went to pieces!" But it hadn't. We took it to the shipyard to get the damage fixed. After we got it fixed up, we took out the old engine and put in a new 100-horsepower Caterpillar diesel.

The boat was almost done. I noticed a boat I had never seen before, the *Tordenskjold*, out of Seattle, lying alongside the New

England Fish Company dock in Astoria. It had flags and barrels and anchors and miles of line and all kinds of nets with six-inch glass balls and a whole deck of gear. We looked at each other and said, "What the heck is he going after?" He had just come in to get fuel, so he took off and was gone about a week or ten days, when he was back. I saw him coming in the river as we were just going out. His bow was way down, loaded with something. We turned around and went back to see what he had.

He went to New England Fish with a boat full of sharks in the round. He had them take the livers out of the sharks, and they just dumped the shark because they couldn't sell them. They were probably pretty old, too. But they got eleven 50-gallon drums full of the livers from those sharks. And for those livers they got $44,000. The livers were a rich source of Vitamin A, which couldn't be made synthetically then. During the war, there was a big need for Vitamin A for the pilots, because this vitamin enhances night vision.

When I saw that, I told my brother, "My gosh, look at that! We couldn't gross $44,000 in a whole year dragging. We'd better look into this thing." I bought some of the linen gillnets they use in the Columbia. They're about sixty meshes deep. But then we found out that the *Tordenskjold* had nets only twenty-two meshes deep and ten-inch mesh with glass balls on the cork line and leads for the bottom. We tried to get the glass balls like he had, but no one had ever heard of them. And we couldn't buy the netting he had either. He had cotton netting and we just had old linen gill netting.

I was single then and so I asked my girlfriend to cap a bunch of empty quart beer bottles. We got cases and cases of empties and she capped them and we tied them on the cork line as floats just as though they were six-inch glass balls.

We went out off Seaside with the *Elector* and this sixty-mesh gillnet for shark nets. We didn't have very much of it, maybe three hundred fathom or so, just enough to try it out. We didn't have any way to lay it out, and we were afraid we would break our beer bottles, so we just laid it out in the wind and let the wind blow the boat sideways. Very slowly the net went out as the wind blew. At that time we wanted to fish on the bottom so we put an anchor on one end and another anchor on the other end, and then we had a ball, a barrel and a flag on each end so we could see the ends of the net. At last we got it on the bottom and got the anchors out.

We let it stay out there for a few days. We didn't even have a puller to get the net back in again. So we came in to have one made. When we went back out, by golly, we had two or three sharks in there, but you couldn't see the fish. You could see the shape in the net, but it was so wrapped up in the linen net, you couldn't even see it. I said, "This will never do. My gosh, it took us fifteen to twenty minutes to get one fish out." We decided we couldn't use the linen nets. We ordered new gear from Seattle, and found some round glass balls and went into the shark business the right way.

~

With our new gear we'd put out in about seventy fathom. We had pretty close to a mile of gear. It was best to lay out the net before a storm and then go out and get it after the weather cleared again. If you had your shark gear out there with no storm, just flat water, you might get four or five sharks, but if there was a storm, you might get a hundred. After a storm we would start in the morning and we'd work all day and maybe all night to get all the nets in. It took that long to lift them. We were getting eight dollars a pound for the liver and every fish had five pounds of liver. That's about forty bucks for each shark.

While we were fishing shark, we would also catch some ling cod, so we accumulated those livers, too. We had the *Elector* and the *Coolidge II* fishing together so we had quite a few cod livers. We decided we would sell them. We usually got a dollar a pound for them. I took them to New England Fish. They tested them and said they would give us twenty cents a pound. I told them I would let them rot in the freezer before I would sell to them for twenty cents.

I called Bioproducts in Hammond and asked if they were interested. They said they would be happy to test them and give me a bid. So they did. They called me a week later and told me they would give me $14.40 a pound. I almost fell off my chair. I couldn't believe it. I said I would be right down. I couldn't get there fast enough. They said they had tested them three times. We had about thirty

George with soupfin shark.

pounds of livers, so the two boats split the money and we were really happy. I showed the check to the New England fish people and
they couldn't believe it, either.

One day after a storm we went out on the *Elector*. We had one big
long string of nets from southwest of the lightship toward Tillamook
Rock. We came to lift our nets and saw a boat coming toward us.
There are guys who go up and down the coast. If they see a boat
offshore, they go to see what's going on because they're looking
for sharks also. I saw this boat coming. We had about thirty to forty
sharks on deck in the bow where we had just thrown them. Our
puller was back aft and we had a roller on the bow so that we'd
pick up the net from right near the anchor. You could see the fish
coming in the net because they have white bellies and the water is
clear there. Just when this boat started coming, we could see four
or five fish below the surface. We shut the engine down and let the
net back so they couldn't see these fish down underwater. The guy
came up to us and said, "How're you doin'?" We had taken all but
one of the sharks off the deck and thrown them in the fish hold. We
held up this one fish and said, "Well, we got one here." So he looked
at it and I said, "Where've you been?" "Oh, we just came out of
Seattle and are running down the coast and haven't found anything

Coolidge II with floating soupfin shark gear on deck.

yet." Then he asked, "Why don't you have your engine running? What's wrong?" I said, "Oh, the engine got hot and we had to let her cool off before we can start it again." And off he went. After he got a couple miles away, we started picking up again.

We ended up with about $5,000 worth of shark that set. If we had told him what we had, he most likely would have laid out right down in front of us. If you have a good spot, you have to keep it to yourself. It's just like a gold mine. You don't tell anybody where you're getting them because they'll follow you and put their nets right on top of yours. And that's the way it works. So anyway, we went in and delivered.

The boat that had come out to see what we were doing was the *Coolidge II*. Just two years later we wound up buying that boat. It was up for sale. Some guy in Ilwaco had bought it and I had a chance to get it from him. I talked to Henry Goodrich about buying the boat for me. I really wanted it. It was seventy feet long and a lot better than the *Elector*. Mr. Goodrich told his right hand man to see that I got the boat. We went up to the First National Bank and borrowed all the money I could get. So, in 1944 I bought her. It had an old Enterprise diesel engine in it. We made a trip into Canada to Rose Spit. We spent two weeks fishing dogfish for the livers. On the way back, just when I slowed her down to come into the basin in Astoria, the crankshaft broke. So we had to buy a new engine and got a V-8 Caterpillar. There was this fellow who was going to be my engineer. I told him, "Now we're going to take this old engine out and put in a Cat. I'll take the other boat, the *Elector* and tow the *Coolidge II* over to the Columbia Boat shop." They had some pilings sticking up, so we tied the boat to the piling so it would stay straight up when the tide went out. The engineer and I took the heads off the old engine and put it on one side, but the boat was leaning the wrong way, so I said to him, "Let me give you a hand. We'll carry these heads over on the opposite side so the boat slants a little bit toward the piling so it won't tip over." But he said, "Go, get out of here! I'll take care of everything. I've put hundreds of boats on the beach. You just take the other boat back where you got it and leave me here."

He was going to stay on the boat all night and we were going to change the propeller in the morning at low tide. I wanted to change the pitch of the propeller so it would take care of the bigger engine we were putting in. When he told me to go and let him take care of everything, I trusted him. I shouldn't have. When I came back in the morning, the boat had fallen over. It pulled out the two pilings we had tied up to, and the boat was lying on its side with the engine loose in the hold. I said to him, "Yeah! It looks like you've put hundreds of boats on the beach. Look at that. Look at it." He didn't say a thing. But it just goes to show you, don't trust a guy that knows everything. I found that out.

We did get the boat out of there. The fall had bent the valve cover and did a little damage to the engine, but not too much. We were getting ready to put a bait tank on and go fishing for tuna. The engineer said (the same guy now), "Well, I want the corner rack." He had been fishing tuna before. He knew the corner rack on a bait tank boat is the hottest rack. When the bait is thrown out to attract the tuna, the corner sticks out further so he gets a better chance. I told him, "Okay, you can have the corner rack." We got our bait and went out to sea. We had to run out sixty to seventy miles offshore to find the tuna. We got into a school of tuna and that engineer on the corner rack started throwing tuna. He did get more than anyone else, but he started complaining, "Oh! My back! My back! I can't do it!" So I said to him, "Okay. You take the next rack, right next to you on the stern." So he took the next rack, and then he started to get into an argument with the chummer because now he wasn't getting enough fish. I actually thought he was going to get into a fight over it. He said, "You're not chumming it right." I said, "No fighting on the boat. I'm going to take you guys in if you're going to fight." He was never satisfied. Now I had learned something else. Watch the guy that brags.

We were off Coos Bay for tuna. We had used up our bait and had to run in to get more. Bait only lasts a couple of days or so and you have to go back to the beach to catch more. I found a little spot there but we didn't see any sign of bait. We laid out "in the blind," put the bait net out in a circle and pulled it back in, and, by golly, we got twenty scoops of bait. I thought to myself, "Gee, that's pretty good. We never saw a fish and yet they were there." So we put those in the tank and made seven to eight sets, and, by golly, we got all the bait we wanted.

A fellow by the name of Dan Luketa was fishing with the *Sunbeam* out of Seattle. He came over and said, "How are you getting that bait? Do you see anything?" I said, "Oh, yeah! We see it all over here." I had to lie to him. I did not want him to know we were laying out in the blind as he might take our spot and then we wouldn't be able to fish. So I had to fool him. I went from one side of the boat to the other, leaned over and said, "Let the net go!" to make him believe I saw a lot of fish.

We went out to sea with our bait and, by golly, I have never seen anything like it. You couldn't run five minutes in one direction until you saw a school of tuna just boiling on top of the water. They were all over the place. It didn't matter which direction you went, you'd see a school of fish. We got about six to seven ton of fish, and that was pretty good because we were new at the game. The next day she blew up a storm so we had to go back to Astoria. That was the end of the season, but I sure enjoyed that day. Then we took the tank off and got ready to go dragging and sharking.

We took the boat down to Cape Blanco to fish sharks down that way and then on to San Francisco. The sharks are on the bottom and also on the surface, so we had both kinds of gear. The surface nets were oh, about five hundred fathom long, and we'd lay it out and tie on one end of it, like a sea anchor. We had big round rubber balls about eighteen inches in diameter tied to the cork line on the shark nets. The top of the net where the glass balls were was about fifty feet below the surface. So, if a ship came by, he wouldn't get the net in his propeller because the net was below the ship's draft.

~

Down around San Francisco we were fishing near the *Argo*, skippered by Fred Welleson. He had come down to fish shark too. There was also a fellow who came out of Monterey by the name of Neil Burton. I forget the name of his boat. Fred called him on the radio and said, "Hey Neil! What are you doing?" He answered, "Oh, I'm hanging onto the end of ten grand." In other words, he was hanging onto the end of ten thousand dollars worth of gear. So they signed off. About an hour later, Fred called him again and said, "Hey Neil! How many balls have you got on your net?" "Oh," he said, "We've got about forty balls." Fred said, "Well, I only count about ten." And boy, Neil got excited. His net had broken in two and drifted away, and he only had a quarter of his net left. He started picking it up. It was blowing pretty good, maybe thirty-five to forty miles per hour northwest. I called him and said, "Gee Neil, don't pick your net. Hang onto it and wait till the weather calms down and maybe you'll find the rest of it because it can't be too far away." But he didn't do that. He picked it up. It was too rough to search for it, so he went on in and called it quits and lost the gear. It was the end of his shark venture.

~

We headed back up toward the Columbia River and started working with a fellow named Einar Rice on the schooner, *Masonic*. He went into Eureka to sell his shark livers and we went in there, too. He came out a day ahead of us and headed up the coast. Then I came out and headed for Cape Blanco. I called Einar and asked, "Where are you?" He said, "I'm off Bondon!" He meant Bandon. I signed off. I didn't want to give away to other boats where he was. When I got up there I called again, "I'm off Bandon, Einar, and I don't see you." "Oh, I'm out on the etch, out on the etch." He meant, "I'm out on the edge where it drops off." It drops off pretty fast below one hundred fathom. I didn't say anything more. I knew he was lying to me.

I had heard about the Cape Blanco rock pile where they catch sharks, so I took a course back to Cape Blanco. Bandon is twenty to thirty miles north of Blanco. Sure enough, there was Einar pulling his gear in the middle of the night. So I said, "How're you doin', Einar?" "Oh, yust getting a few stragglers." And he thought I would just talk to him for a few minutes and then beat it, but I stayed there for about an hour and a half until he picked up that one string of gear. And boy, did he ever have the shark. I think he must have had $4,000 to $5,000 worth of sharks in that string.

I told him, "I'm going to lay my gear out here." He said, "Don't you do it!

I didn't trust him so I told the guy with me, "Go ahead and throw the flag out and the barrel and start laying out." It was about midnight so I put the spotlight out on the bow. There was somebody else's flag and barrel! I said, "I guess he's right. Pull it back in again. We'll anchor up for the night and see what she looks like in the daytime."

When the daylight came, boy, it looked like a checkerboard square. There were lots of flags. If we'd had laid that net out, we would have crossed I don't know how many nets. They were so close together all you could see were flags all over the place. He was right, but I didn't believe him so I had to find out for myself.

I called him again and asked, "Einar, where can we lay out here?" "Well," he said, "There really is no place for you to lay out. The rock pile is full of nets. There is no room for you. There is room to lay out on the edge of the rocks, but you'll lose out on the livers. Those eels out in the mud will crawl into the shark and eat up the liver and the sand fleas are going to eat the rest of the flesh. You'll have nothing but the shark skin and bone, head, and tail."

We had to try it, so we laid out on the edge of the rocks, just clear of the other guys so we wouldn't get tangled up with them. We laid her out, and sure enough, he was right. We got some good sharks, but some were eaten. Where he was, he didn't lose any. So, we had to leave the area. He was right, there was no room for us.

The competition was really bad. I saw the *Seabird* picking his string of nets. He was almost to the end of the string when the *North*

Pacific came and laid his net right where the *Seabird* had been. They were fighting over the same spot. That's the way it was.

We tried to get into Coos Bay but a storm was blowing so we had to stay out in the storm all night long and "jog" at the entrance buoy. The wind was blowing so hard we had to run three-quarter speed just to keep up with the buoy! It sure was a good thing we had that brand new Caterpillar engine in the boat. If we had broken down in that wind, we would have been on the beach as the entrance buoy wasn't too far offshore. By golly, at daylight the breakers on the bar were breaking all the way across, but the swell had come down a little bit. For about twenty minutes the bar looked pretty good, so we thought we'd try it. We got in okay. I was really tickled to be in, as I had been down there at the wheel all night long. The rest of the crew was seasick. It was a tough night, raining and blowing. When the other boats tried to get in a half hour later, they couldn't make it, so they were stuck on the outside jogging for a couple more days before they could make it in.

The next day I called Captain Cleaveland on the *Seabird* to see how he was doing out there in the storm. He said, "We're just jogging along," like it was nothing, but all my boys had been seasick.

George with sharks.

We then went back to the Columbia River and stayed up there. It's better to be close to home. We fished southwest of the lightship for about three years in the same spot. We'd pick up about $25,000 worth of sharks in the wintertime, which is pretty good. We went dragging in the summer. Dragging isn't very good in the wintertime and the weather prevented us from going out anyway, so sharking was a good alternative in the winter.

One time we went out to pick up the shark net, and, by golly, we couldn't find the gear. Sometimes the nets drift if they are left out too long or the storms are too big and the swells too large. We started looking. The current runs north, so I went north, and sure enough, we found it up off the Willapa, which is about twenty miles to the north. We first saw the flag, but the net was all in a ball. The anchors had gotten tangled up with the net; so then they didn't hold anymore, and the whole ball of wax started moving up the coast. We picked it up with the boom, took it to shore and straightened it out there.

Another time we were going out to lift our shark gear that had been out there about a week during a storm. There were ten to fifteen boats trying to get out of the river. It was calm outside but there was a big sea running. Just as we got over the bar, a big wave broke behind us. We got out just in time. The rest of the boats didn't make it and had to call it a day.

We found our gear, picked it up and laid it out again so it was ready for another storm. That's the way we did it in the wintertime. It was a pretty nice deal because we never took our shark gear in. It stayed out there the whole winter. We could go home and sleep while our nets did the fishing. The Seattle fishermen would go out for ten days or more. They would "jog," and wait until it calmed down to pick up their gear. But we did it the easy way. Why go out and beat your brains out when you can go home and sleep? Of course, that meant we didn't fix any holes in the net either. We had holes in our nets big enough to drive a car through, but we just kept on fishing with them. The people in Seattle used to take their nets in and patch every hole and rack them and bluestone them and take care of them. But we never did. We'd try to get a year or two out of them, and then we'd buy new ones.

⌐

Captain John Blum from the *Albatross* was fishing shark outside the Columbia. He came in to sell his livers. He tied his boat alongside the fish dock, and they found the boat, but they couldn't find him. Two days later they found his body under the fish dock. He was a heavy drinker. We guessed he fell off the ladder getting on or off his boat.

CHAPTER 5
Out of the Ashes

By 1950, the tuna fishing fell off around the Astoria area and the Washington and Oregon coasts. There had been a lot of bait boats fishing out of there in 1944–45. They all took their bait tanks off their boats and stored them around the cannery. They thought there would be more tuna fishing some day, but there never was. Those tanks just lay around till they got rusty and were finally hauled to the dump. I bought up a lot of the new bait nets in the marine supply stores. They couldn't sell them, so I got them cheap. Then I hauled them in a trailer down to California and sold them to the bait boats that were down there. While there I visited relatives, so the nets paid for the trip.

In 1951 on one of my "net trips" to California, I saw this burned boat, the *El Padre,* in the shipyard. One Saturday I climbed on board. The house was burned off although the engine looked all right. The hull was pretty good except for the bow. Another fellow was looking around the boat, so I asked him "Do you know anything about this boat?" He said, "Yes, I'm the insurance surveyor." I asked him if the boat was going up for bid and if anyone could bid on it. He said it was and he gave me all the information and who to see. I put up a bid, I think for $5,000. I got the boat. Then I had to figure out where to work on it. I found a place at Twenty-Second Street in San Pedro and rented a dock there. I was lucky to get it because it was about the only place that was private and available. It had just enough space to tie the boat up. We could also drive the car up to it, so it was easy to work on the boat.

The house had burned off completely and all the beams were burned. Standing on the deck you could look down at the engine. I found this fellow by the name of Panky who was a good boat carpenter. He had a little boatyard and a partner by the name of Tony

Cvicharovich. They agreed to fix the boat at a good rate. I thought, "By golly, we'll fix this boat up and take it up to Astoria and go dragging with it." So we went to work. We put some new planks in the bow. The hull was good from the waterline on down.

While we were working on the *El Padre* I heard about another boat, the *Esperia III*, which hit the Long Beach jetty in the fog and sank. I looked at it, and the bottom, from the waterline on down was all smashed in, the propeller shaft was bent; the rudder was all bent, and there were holes all over the hull. The only good things on the boat were the engines, the pilothouse (which had an altar in it), the mast, boom, some deck machinery, and an anchor winch. Those were exactly the things I needed to fix up the *El Padre*. "Boy, if I could have those things, I could really fix up the burned boat in good shape." I put a bid on it and then had a friend of mine put a bid on it. I think I bid $4,500 and my friend put in a lesser bid. If there is only one bid on a boat, they might turn it down. If there are two, they might sell it. So, I got that boat too and I was happy.

The insurance company had the boat brought in from the Long Beach breakwater and put on dry dock. They had to make sure it was an accident before they paid on it. It was an accident, they paid on it, and I bought it from the insurance company. While it was still in the yard, I went to see a house mover in Long Beach about getting the engine out of the boat. I asked him if he could do it. He said, "Can we do it? Do you see that big building over there (about a four- or five-story building)? We moved that. Do you see that tank fifty feet up there? We moved that." He showed me all sorts of pictures of things he had moved. I said, "Well, I guess you're qualified to do this." He looked at my new boat and said, "Well, you're going to have to cut a hole ten feet wide from deck to keel, and then take the engine loose from its base. We'll take it from there." So I got a chain saw and cut the hole, got the engine off its base, and headed it out like he wanted. They came down with a truck and bunch of cribbing. They got a hold of that engine and had it out of there and on their truck in about two hours. I never saw anyone work that fast. Boy, they hollered! Guys were running around piling up the cribbing to move the engine. They yarded it up to the truck with their winch and asked, "Where to?"

A friend of mine had a shop about a mile away so we took it to his shop and stored it there while I was working on the boat. This was a 250-horsepower, 6-cylinder Atlas Imperial diesel, direct reversing, which meant it would run both ways. It was a nice engine, but it had been underwater and I needed to take it apart and get it running. I just left it up in this guy's shop because we were too busy on the boat.

Some guys came up from Mexico. They had broken a crankshaft on their engine and were looking for another one. They heard somewhere that I had this engine, so they came to see me. I was working on the boat and was down to the last few dollars I had. I really had to sell that engine. They looked at the engine all there in pieces, and said they wanted an engine that was running. So they left.

I followed them for the whole day without their knowing it. They went to junkyards and shops, shipyards, looking at engines. They looked at everything that ran. I thought to myself, "Boy! These guys are looking for a price. They don't care what kind of engine they get as long as it runs." I knew I couldn't let these guys get away without buying my engine. I needed this sale. They walked all over. Finally they went to a paint shop in San Pedro. I knew the paint guy because I had done business with him. He could speak Spanish and did a lot of business with Mexicans who would come to him when they wanted to buy things in the United States. He knew the ropes and acted as a go-between. After they had been in the store a few minutes, I walked in. I said to them, "Listen, I've been thinking about the engine. I'll tell you what I'll do. I'll overhaul my engine and get it running if you give me $6,800." They said, "Okay, if we get a mechanic to oversee the job and see that it's done right."

I didn't have time to fix the engine myself, so I went to the White Engine Company on Terminal Island and hired a couple of guys who wanted extra money on the side to do this on the weekend. Coincidentally, the paint guy went to the same company to hire a mechanic to oversee the job. He ended up hiring the boss of the two I had hired to oversee two of his own workers. The two workers hadn't planned on telling their boss so it was a problem for them. But it turned out just fine. The boss, Roy Koots, ended up helping the two guys put this engine together in two days. They put her on skids, started her up, everything checked out, and shipped her off. And I got my $6800 to finish working on my boat.

Those were tough days. Fishing was poor in California. Guys were going broke and sinking their boats on purpose or burning them up just to collect from the insurance company. We heard all kinds of stories. Nobody wanted to buy boats.

We had to get the pilothouse off the *Esperia III*. I told the yard, "I want to hire a man with a chain saw for half a day. I want to cut the pilothouse loose from the hull." So I hired this guy to cut the beams off the very ends where they're bolted to the shelf on the boat so there would still be part of the deck under the house. When it was loose it could be lifted off the boat. For buoyancy, I put about twenty empty oil drums in the engine room and emptied the fuel tanks and plugged all the fuel outlets. Then we launched the boat and towed it over to a *stiff leg*, something like a stationary crane. It swung out from the dock and, with a sling around the house, picked it up and put her ashore.

We bolted new beams alongside the old ones to reach across the *El Padre*. Then with the stiff leg we picked the house up and put it on the *El Padre*. And after we got it in place, you wouldn't know it wasn't built that way.

We just got her fixed up, and a Mexican came looking for a boat to buy. I thought it might be a pretty good deal for me. So we sold it for $40,000. With that, I figured I had just paid myself $10,000 for a year's work. Not bad! It was a lot of good experience for me. So they took off with the boat down to Mexico.

After I sold the *El Padre* there was another burned boat. The insurance company had it on the same dry dock I had found the *Esperia III*. This was the *Aurora*, a nice big 85-footer with a 22-foot beam. It had a 235-horsepower Union diesel in it, with direct reversing.

I thought maybe I'd been paying too much for these boats. I didn't really care if I got this one or not, so I put in a really low bid, only $1,850 on this one. I had another guy put in another bid, a little lower than I had, so there would be the two bids. And, by golly, I got it for $1,850. I was really tickled.

There had been an explosion in the bow and it had pushed the planks about two inches out from the stem. I had the shipyard fix that part so it would float when they took it off dry dock. Everything was perfect from the waterline down, so we moved it to our rented dock. The boat had a double house on it. One was little, with a bunk and a chart room. We moved this house and put it aft so we could rebuild the under house. Although the sides were good, much of this house had to be renewed with new bunks and a new stove. We put a new roof on it and then put the pilothouse back on again, and, gee, it came out pretty good.

I had intended to take this boat up to Astoria for dragging. One of the fellows who was working for me said, "Why don't you fix this boat up for tuna? It will hold 115 ton and it's ideal." I said, "Maybe you have something there." So we started working on getting it ready for tuna fishing.

One Saturday one of the fish packers was driving by and saw the boat while we were working on it. He came over and asked what I was going to do with the boat. I told him I was fixing it up for tuna but I was running out of money and needed some help. This guy had a fish plant on Terminal Island and told me to come see him. The next day, a Sunday, a guy I knew from Starkist came by and asked me what I was doing. I told him the same thing, but that I was going to borrow money from the guy next door to him.

He said, "You come and see me Monday and we'll see what we can do." I preferred to borrow from Starkist because it was a bigger outfit and they would have a better chance to help me than the guy with a smaller plant. So I went over to Starkist and he wrote me a check for $5,000. I started buying equipment and everything I needed. I just signed a note for it. When we had used up that money he loaned me $8,000 more and we used that up too, so he put me on an open account for anything I wanted to buy. I just charged it to them. I fixed it as cheaply as I could because I didn't want to get too far in debt to Starkist.

Times were tough. One time when I was in the Starkist office I saw three or four guys sitting there on a bench waiting to see the president of the company. The receptionist was right there. She had

Full Load
sF Bottom
Fish AST. OR.
1950

Georgene M with bottom fish being unloaded at the New England Fish Company, Astoria.

told the boss who was waiting for him and that they wanted to borrow money. He didn't want to see them, so they sat there all day. About 4:30 p.m. they asked the receptionist again to see the boss. "Oh, he left!" They would come back the next day and the same thing would happen. If the company knew you wanted to borrow money, they wouldn't talk to you. The fish packers were having a hard time, too.

We got the boat done and, gee, it looked pretty good. The company said, "We'll get a skipper for you and take it down to Mexico, to purse seine for tuna." The first year they had the boat, there was this guy who got all his gear and net on the boat and went to make a test set at Point Firman. That's right off Pedro, in deep water. Most skippers make a test set to make sure all the machinery works well and the net is in good shape. This guy laid out his net and made a circle with it. The skiff man threw the line up on the boat but the guy on the boat lost the line to the net, and boy, that skipper got all excited. The net started to sink as the guy had lost the end of the net so he had to go back and get a hold of it, maybe fifteen fathom from the end because it was going down slowly. He grabbed the cork line and saved it. They could have lost the whole net and it probably cost

$20,000. Once it starts sinking, the net won't float. You have to have a boat on each end.

They left for Mexico to go for tuna. There were refrigeration coils in the hold. I don't think the coils would really freeze the fish. They just helped keep the ice from melting. They went, but they didn't make a dime, even though they had it for a year. They hired another skipper and he had it for a year and they still didn't make anything. These were good skippers, but tuna fishing was bad and times were tough. The company was tight with money and wouldn't give them money to fix their nets or for their own use.

⌒

Five years went by and they never paid a dime on the boat. They called me in Astoria where I was dragging and told me to come down because they were foreclosing on my boat. They said, "You owe us $42,000 and you haven't paid a dime on the mortgage and we just can't carry you any longer. We need the money." I asked if they would discount the mortgage. And they said, "We'll discount it a thousand dollars." I said, "One thousand dollars! That's nothing!" So the man asked me to wait a minute while he went to talk to somebody. He came back and offered to discount it $6,000. I said, "That's more like it. With $6,000 off, I'll buy it." I couldn't. I was broke. There was no way I could buy it! I was just making ends meet. But I told him I'd buy it because I figured the boat wasn't do-ing anything and they'd hire some other skipper to go fish sardines instead of tuna. In that way, they would get the boat working and wouldn't foreclose. But, they didn't. They didn't hire anybody and they left it there and called back in two weeks and asked where the $36,000 was for the boat. I told them I would be down.

I went down there and talked to them, "Look, I sold my other boat and got all my money in this one." I had about $70,000 in this boat and here we were going to sell it for $36,000." They said, "Well, that's the price, but we have a partner for you." I said no at first. "You're not going to get by with this. No millionaire is going to take this boat away from me, only over my dead body. I put a lot of work in this boat and it wasn't my fault it didn't make any money. If I were running the boat, then I could understand it, but you hired all the skippers and are now blaming it on me! No way! It isn't right!"

Finally they said, "Okay, we'll work it out!" That's exactly what I wanted them to do. So they said, "We've got a partner for you with $10,000 to put into it. He is a good man and we're going to back him up." I agreed.

So, after I had been back in Astoria about a week, he called me and said, "Hey, we've got a man here who's got a new spray system for freezing tuna. He wants to put it on your boat because it's just the size he wants." In other words, mine was a good boat to experiment with. This guy's name was Mike Newell. Starkist was going to give him $5,000 to put this system on the boat, and he was confident it would work. Although the cannery wasn't too excited about it, they were going to back him up. If the patent worked out, the company was going to have 51 percent. The engineer and the skipper were going to have the other 49 percent between them. So they agreed.

They had to fiberglass the hold and make it watertight, and they had to put in a refrigeration system. It was going to cost quite a bit of money. So they wanted me to give half of my half to the engineer. He was the guy who thought he was going to get a patent on this system. I said, "No way. I'm not going to give anything away. I've lost enough here already. But, I'll tell you what I will do. We'll give him 20 percent. I'll give him 10 percent and my partner can give him 10 percent." So they said, "Well, that sounds all right. Here's the way it's going to be. If the system works, this guy will get 20 percent of the boat free and clear of all the bills. And if it doesn't work, then he will pay 20 percent of the $36,000 owing." I said that was good enough for me.

So we made a deal and he put the spray system in the boat and it worked really well. There were pipes overhead and pipes down the side and around the whole fish hold so you'd put a few thousand gallons of water in the boat. When the boat got full of tuna, the fish would be sprayed. There was salt in the water so it wouldn't freeze, but it would freeze the fish. It worked really well. Then everybody in the fleet started to steal this system. They saw how it was put in. But this guy didn't have a patent on it. They wouldn't give him a patent, so they all stole it and used it for nothing.

That guy didn't come out very well at all, so he started to sue some of the guys who had stolen his system. He wanted 5 percent of the take for using his idea. But the fishermen didn't want to pay it. I told him one day, "Why don't you take 2 percent? If you took 2 percent and let the association handle it for you (everybody belonged to the association), you could give them half of a percent for collecting it and you'd have money coming in your mailbox without doing much. Just hire a good lawyer and go over there and have a meeting. The boys, instead of stealing your system, would rather pay you 2 percent." But, he went for the 5 percent and he lost the case, so he didn't get anything.

My new partner had a buddy who was a pilot who used to spot tuna with airplanes and then notify the skipper so he could be on the tuna first. He did real well and paid off the mortgage.

Each of those five years I was dealing with Starkist, June and I, with our four daughters, went down to San Pedro to see what was going on. One year I drove up to the boat and there was the sheriff sitting on my boat. I didn't tell him who I was, but hollered down, "What's the scoop on this thing?" "Oh," he said, "Some guy came down from the mast at night and stepped through the glass on top of the freezer. He got cut pretty badly and he's suing the boat."

I called Starkist and asked, "What's going on here?" "Well, this guy's hurt and he's suing for the full price of the boat. But it's been going on here for quite a while. We were going to settle in a few days, but I wouldn't go near the boat if I were you. They might take your car and everything you have if they find out you own the boat." So, I went down to Mexico for a few days. When I came back they had it all settled.

This was about the time they began building the big 600-ton tuna seiners. The bait boat fleet was centered in San Diego, but the purse seine fleet was in San Pedro. The seiner fleet was dominated by the Slavonians. The Portuguese had the big boats and they knew all the areas to fish in South America and in Panama, but they didn't know how to purse seine, so they hired the Slavs either to run their boats or be deck bosses for them. They built these big seiners in Tacoma, 600-tonners, 1,200-tonners, and even 2,000-tonners (the capacity of the tuna they could hold).

Some of these big boats had helicopters on top of the pilothouse. They'd use the helicopters to look for the tuna, and then

Georgene M at Point Arena, a total loss.

the boats would run out to the tuna. The porpoise ran with the tuna, so when they set on the tuna they got a lot of porpoise with them. The porpoise would run full speed into the net and they'd kill themselves hitting the net. So there was a big stink about killing the porpoise. People stopped buying tuna because of the porpoise and the whole industry went to pot in our country. All the canneries in San Pedro went out of business. A bunch of fishermen bought Starkist, but they couldn't handle it either. The porpoise issue ruined it for them. Now there aren't any canneries in San Diego or San Pedro. So, the boats started fishing in foreign countries where they didn't have such tough laws. The whole fleet moved down to Australia, New Zealand, and the South Pacific. Times change and things change.

While in San Pedro in 1952, I ran into a guy named Art Nelson who had run the *New Zealand* up in Bristol Bay. We had chartered it out as a salmon tender and he was the skipper. So I asked him if he wanted to run a boat for me. He asked me what I had, and I told him about a 65-foot, all-steel boat with a new engine I had in Astoria named the *Georgene M.* after my oldest daughter. He said he would bring it down to Pedro and rig and run it for jigging tuna.

We had gone down to Tijuana and Ensenada, Mexico, for the day by car. Just as we walked back in the house the phone rang. The voice on the phone said there was a fellow by the name of Art Nelson who wanted to talk to me because his boat just went on the beach. It was in the breakers, a mile and a half north of the Point Arena light in California.

So I grabbed a plane and went up to San Francisco, rented a car at the airport, and went out to see what the deal was. I had called the insurance company and told them the boat was on the beach, so they sent a surveyor to take a look. We arrived at the same time. He said, "As far as we're concerned, it's a total loss. We're not even going to try to get it off the beach. You only have $20,000 of insurance on it, and it would cost more than that to salvage it." So I asked him if he would sell the boat, just as it was. He said he would. I asked how much, and he asked how much I would pay. I told him $500 and he said, "Sold!" So I told him to take it out of the insurance money he was going to pay me.

So, I had my boat back. It was leaning out toward the sea. All the breakers came up and washed the deck. I wanted to put a line on it and pull the boat over with a bulldozer so the mast leaned against the shore. I figured then I could save the boat. My plan was to get a pump mounted on the deck and pump the water out of it so a bulldozer could pull it way up on the beach at high tide. So I contacted this guy who had bulldozers and told him I wanted two bulldozers, a D8 and a D6. He promised he would be there at low tide the next morning. He came down, but only with the little one, the D6. With that we could hardly budge it.

When we couldn't do anything with the bulldozer, I figured I'd take the engine out and junk the rest. It was a brand new engine, a 200-horsepower 6-110 General Motors engine. I don't think it even had 250 hours on it. I told the skipper that I was going to get that engine out. He told me, "You might as well come to Pedro with me, because you ain't going to get it out." I told him, "You don't know me. I'll have that engine up on the beach." I didn't know whether I could or not, but I told him I could.

I went to a fellow who had a little machine and welding shop not too far away from the boat. I asked him if he wanted a job. I told

Georgene M at Point Arena with whole cut in the sisde to remove the engine.

him I had a steel boat on the beach and I wanted him to cut a hole in it and take the engine out. I told him I wanted two tanks, one for each of us because we only had three hours to get the engine out. So I cut a hole in the hull, just to look in. It was right by the gas tank for the auxiliaries, starting engines, charging batteries and so forth. I didn't know if the skipper had any gas in that tank or not, but the hose was on fire. The whole engine room was on fire—even the hose going to the deck we used to fill gas in the tank. Oil had leaked out and the whole engine room had gone up in flames.

A fellow came along on a horse. He was just curious. I said, "Hey, how about going up there and getting a fire extinguisher. There's one up there on the beach." So he went up to get the fire extinguisher. In the meantime I took some sand and threw in the hole we had cut in the side of the boat, and, by golly, when we threw the sand in there, part of the fire went out. Oil was burning on top of the water, so all three of us started throwing sand in there and we got the fire out before the guy came back with the extinguisher.

Then I tried to make a deal with the guy who had brought down the tanks. I said, "Look! We've got to really step on it because the tide's coming in pretty soon. We'll be stuck and not get it out of there. We've got to really speed up on this thing. I'll give you $300 or nothing. If we get the engine out, you get 300 bucks. Otherwise, you only get an hourly wage." But the guy turned it down. "I'll take the six dollars an hour." He needed the money and wasn't willing to gamble. So, we went ahead and started working and cutting. We got a hole cut big enough to get the engine out.

My brother Jack was there, so I told him to take the bolts loose on the shaft, and I'd take the engine bed bolts out. I figured I would do that because I had put the engine in and knew where they were, even under water. We had our heads above water and then had to reach down as far as we could with our hands to undo the bolts. We finally got her all loose. We had come-alongs to slide the engine off the bed and cut a big slab off the side of the boat and laid the engine on top of this. Then the bulldozer pulled the engine up on the beach. We filled it up with diesel fuel so it wouldn't rust from the salt water. I had a truck come up from Berkeley to take the engine down there. They took it all apart and overhauled it, because it had been in salt water. It cost about a thousand dollars, but I had a good engine. I left the engine there until I needed it. We also retrieved a Sperrey automatic pilot, and a lot of the radio gear, which made the $500 I paid for it a real bargain. There were big swells on this beach. They tore the whole pilothouse off the deck and it didn't take long for the sea to beat her to pieces.

Bidding on a boat is easy but the competition is another matter. This was particularly true in 1981 when I wanted to buy a 68-foot shrimper, the *Taasinge*. It had a 360 H.P. Cat diesel in good shape. I bid $3,650 on it. It had burned. After sending my check to the insurance company, I hired two guys to go to Ilwaco to begin cleaning it up. I had them start by cleaning up the engine room. I had just gotten there when the former owner came down and told me to get off the boat. He said he wasn't selling this boat to anyone because he hadn't been paid for the loss by the insurance company. I got off the boat and went to Bellingham for a week. When I came back, some of the equipment on the boat was missing. The main hydraulic pump on the front of the engine was missing, as well as the Hyd motor on the net reel. These were two of the most expensive hydraulic items. I called the insurance company who said they could put the vessel up for bid again. I asked a few people about this without getting any good answers. So, I decided to go to Seattle and put in a claim against the insurance company. Even though those two items were worth over $1,500, I put in a claim for $1,000, the limit for small claims court. I won. The owner got paid for his loss, but now I had to get the title. I went to the owner and he refused to give it to me until I gave him the ten fifty-gallon drums that were on the boat when it was in Ilwaco. So I did it, got my $1,000 from the insurance, but then they told me those drums belonged to me. So I went to the shipyard and got the drums back.

I finally got the legal papers after about three trips, and started to work on the boat. I had it towed to Warrenton boatyard and had it put on dry dock. I repaired the bottom and then put it back in the water and did the rest of the work while it was tied up alongside the dock. I bought an aluminum pilothouse from the Ilwaco shipyard for $500, cut it in half lengthwise, and made it thirty-eight inches wider to fit the hull and eight feet longer. I took in a partner to put the house on the boat. He was a good aluminum welder and did a fantastic job. It really came out nicely. I named it *Four Daughters* in honor of our four girls. It took about four-and-a-half years to finally get it ready to sell. But I sold it for $45,000.

CHAPTER 6

A New Hope

I heard about a boat for sale in San Francisco by the name of *New Hope*. I thought it looked like a nice boat. But down on the docks in San Pedro some guys were talking about the boat. One of the guys had turned the boat back because it had stack fires. He said flames would shoot up a good ten feet above the boat and he was afraid all the sparks might catch the nets on fire, so he turned the boat back to the bank. He had been rebuilding the engine and it was all apart in the fish hold.

I found out who was in control of the boat, a bank in Monterey. I went up there and offered them $11,500 for the boat. They took it! I was real happy because this was an 82-foot, 21.5-foot beam boat. It had a Fairbanks Morris diesel in it, which was direct reversible. I didn't know anything about this engine, so I went to the Fairbanks

New Hope with 290 HP Cat diesel in the Columbia River near Astoria.

people and asked them what it would take to put this engine in shape. They told me I had to put in one piston and one cylinder to get her running. They said it would cost about $450 for each. I thought that sounded good. I had in my mind I could take that old Fairbanks out and put in the 6–110 Jimmy that we had just salvaged and overhauled. It wasn't as big as the Fairbanks, but I figured it would push the boat at about eight knots, which was good enough. But the Fairbanks people talked me into keeping their engine.

I was driving down the Bayshore Highway, which, in the fifties, had a lot of surplus stores. I saw this big box in front of one of them, marked 35 F10. That was the identification of the engine I had in the boat. So I asked them what they wanted for that engine kit. It was a whole set of six cylinders and pistons. They wanted $2,500 but I talked them down to $1,800, bought it, and took it over to the boat. We had it tied up to a dock that was not used much.

I worked with a Fairbanks mechanic who had been with the firm for twenty years or so, an old timer. He was on one side of the engine and I was on the other. We had big wrenches and took these big bolts off the connecting rods. They were about an inch and a quarter thick and held the bearings together. It was a really big, husky engine. The crankshaft was inches inches in diameter. We worked five days a week and it took us a month to put this engine back together, to put all the new cylinders on, and to put in the new pistons and rings. But we got her back in shape. When we got done we took her out for a test run and, gee, she made a lot of noise. I told the mechanic there was a whole lot of knocking going on down in the engine room. The mechanic said it was just a fuel knock. We took her over to the dock, put in a new injector, started her up, and it was the same thing. It sounded just like metal to metal. So, we took off the base plate and looked in there and a pile of smoke came out. We had burned the bearing and roughed up the shaft pretty good. The guy told me he wasn't able to work any longer on the engine because he was past due for his vacation, but he would send down another guy. So this other guy came down and he had grinding compound and some files. He worked on that crankshaft for about a day, and, by golly, he got her in good shape–nice and smooth. I wouldn't have believed he could do that with some com- pound and hand tools. We put her back together, ready for another test run. I think this was on a Friday. Monday morning I went to the shop and told them I was ready to go for the test run. They told me they couldn't do that because they were on strike. They said they'd get in big trouble if they went down to the dock and did any work.

So I decided to tie it alongside the dock and test it there myself. I put a good heavy line around the dock piling, started her up, and ran her for five minutes. I put my hand on the bearings and they felt good. I ran her for ten minutes, put my hand on the bearings again, and they still felt good. Then I ran it another fifteen minutes, right there at the dock. The propeller was going ahead, putting a strain on the engine. I sped her up a little more and ran it for fifteen minutes more, and it seemed to be running okay. I couldn't afford to lay in San Francisco anymore, and as long as the engine was run- ning okay, I was going to Astoria. So we left the dock, taking about seventy-five gallons of lube oil in the tank. We had plenty of fuel to get to Astoria.

We ran out as far as the lightship, maybe an hour and a half, and we had used a gallon and a half of lube oil. I knew at that rate, we'd never make it to Astoria. I had noticed when we first started the engine, the oil pressure gauge showed two and a half pounds. The book said the engine needed eight pounds of oil pressure. So, we adjusted it up to eight pounds of pressure. We also noticed the exhaust pipe must have had a leak. The exhaust went to the top, through the stack, and out as dry exhaust. But oil started dripping down from the exhaust. The exhaust pipe was about eight inches in diameter, with tin around that and a lot of insulation so we couldn't see where the leak was. It leaked onto the tin insulation and then ran down and dropped on top of the engine where there was a lot of oil. So I got a five-gallon can and started collecting this oil. It was all coming in one spot. There was nothing wrong with it. It was black, but it was brand new oil. So, we started putting it back in the engine.

I didn't know much about this. I was just going by the book. I thought maybe we'd try to run the oil pressure at five pounds, so I adjusted it from eight to five. It dripped less, but it still dripped. So I put it down to four pounds. It still ran and there was less dripping. We still collected any oil that dripped and put it back in the engine because we couldn't lose any oil. So, I figured we'd turn it down to three pounds and that would be as far as we would go. The gauge showed two and a half pounds and I wanted to have a half-pound of safety there. We ran all the way up to Astoria by putting all the oil back into the engine.

Then we started dragging out of Astoria. The very first day we were out, we burnt a bearing. I knew something about putting bearings in, scraping them in and fitting them. We had an extra bearing and some compound that would smooth the babbit after we put the new bearing in. You have to fit these bearings to the shaft. They weigh about fifty pounds. I put it in out at sea and got the boat running again. We made a couple more trips and burnt another bearing. I knew we couldn't have trouble like this and keep on fishing. I called the Fairbanks people down in San Francisco and complained about the bearings. I told them they must have done a bad job on the engine. They told me this engine had burnt a lot of bearings and they had sent their best mechanics to work on it but they couldn't get a bearing to stay in the engine more than five or six weeks.

I was upset because if I had known this I wouldn't have bought the cylinder kit and put this engine in the boat. I would have put my 6-110 in the boat. So I asked them what they were going to do about it. They told me they would send a man from Seattle for one day free of charge. I thought to myself, "One man, one day! He couldn't do anything for me in that time." But I agreed. So they sent the guy down from Seattle. He'd been with Fairbanks Morris for thirty years. He took one bearing off, looked at it and told me the bearings were babbited wrong. They shim these bearings so you don't get it too tight. There was supposed to be ten- or fifteen-thousandths clearance for oil. That meant the bearings had to be rebabbited so the oil couldn't escape. The oil was going out the shims as the shims were not tight against the shaft. This explained the loss of oil.

We called the Fairbanks people in San Francisco, told them what the problem was, and they agreed to furnish new bearings and rebabbit all the bearings, but they wouldn't put them in. I was going to have to do that. I told them, "No way! If you don't put it in and fix it right, I'm going to sue you for damages." Finally they agreed. They sent a man from Seattle to do the job. He stayed at our house, and the two of us worked for a whole month to fix that engine the way it was supposed to be. We rebabbited all the bearings, put it back together, went out for a test run, but it used just as much oil as before. The mechanic couldn't believe it. He had been with Fairbanks for thirty years and had never had this happen before. Now I was really in a jam.

꙱

I had a chance to charter the boat to Alaska to tender for salmon for Pacific American Fisheries in Bellingham. I took the charter and I went as engineer. We were in the Squaw Harbor area, right in the Shumagin Islands, tendering for King Cove where the cannery was. We'd pick fish up from the Shumagin Island area and haul them over to King Cove to be canned. We got through the whole season with no bearing trouble, and we were up there for seventy days, but we did use a fifty-gallon drum of oil every week. Every time we'd come in to the oil dock, the guy would say, "Roll out the barrel!" We did go through it, but using that much oil created stack fires. This was the problem the guy was having when he turned the boat back. We understood now what the stack fires were from. We had one on the way up to Alaska.

The muffler was about six feet long and about four feet wide and about four feet high. The exhaust went in there. The oil with the exhaust accumulated, stuck to the sides of the muffler, and got so thick, about every ten days there would be a stack fire. We had several of them, but we knew how to handle it, and we got by.

The next year I didn't go. We still had the charter with PAF, which was worth $11,000 for seventy days, which I didn't want to lose. I had another boat in Astoria, so I stayed home and ran that and sent another guy to be engineer on the chartered boat. They got by that year too, but he had to pull a piston while they were there. The company told me after these four years they didn't want to charter my boat anymore because there was too much engine trouble and they couldn't afford the down time. So I made them a deal. They'd

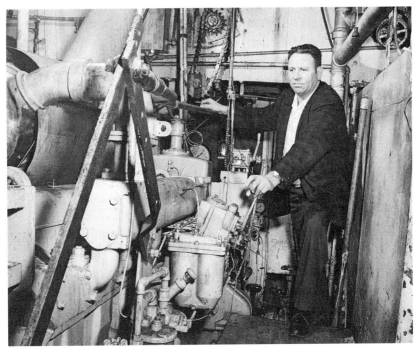

George with a new Cat engine in the *New Hope*.

charter the boat again if I would put in a new Caterpillar turbo-charged engine. So we did. We pulled out that Fairbanks and put in a Diesel 353 Cat 6-cylinder, turbo-charged engine. This new engine ran like a sewing machine.

While we were making the engine swap, we were refrigerating the fish hold and putting in a chilled sea water system so the salmon would keep longer. Now, instead of icing down the fish, they'd just throw them in chilled seawater. The refrigeration could set the temperature at any level you wanted. We'd fill the fish hold full of water. It set the boat way down. It left only about a foot of free board after the boat was loaded with water or salmon, either one. This kept the fish just so they wouldn't freeze and in first-class condition.

This was a major project. We had to fiberglass the entire fish hold. We nailed clean quarter-inch plywood over the inside skin of the ship and then we fiberglassed over the plywood. We all worked hard on this, using two fifty-gallon drums of fiberglass resin. It was a sticky mess. PAF paid for this system. It cost $25,000. But it made a wonderful fish tender and we kept chartering the boat to them.

～

When these jobs were completed I hired an engineer to go north with the boat. He filled the hold with water to check out the new system. When he pumped out the water in the hold, it created such a vacuum that it pulled all the plywood off the ceiling and broke the seal. This was the rubber seal around the entrance hatch into which we threw the salmon. The seal made it airtight. It didn't have an air vent either, so when the engineer was pumping out all that water, it just ripped that plywood right off the ceiling.

There was a lot of damage and it took four men a whole day to do the repairs. We shouldn't have had the rubber seal on the hatch cover. We got it done and the *New Hope* left for Alaska. Everything worked for the entire salmon season.

～

While on the *New Hope* off the Washington Coast, I passed the *Brookfield* going the other way. I looked back and Stein Alsos, the skipper, was on the stern, waving at me. When we passed, we had tangled drag doors. I had a new D 353 Cat diesel in the *New Hope* and was pulling the *Brookfield* backwards. I didn't even realize it. We each pulled our gear in, and boy what a mess it was. It took a long time to get it straightened out.

～

Another time I went down to the dock when I had the *New Hope*, and it wasn't there! No boat! I told my engineer to go one way, down near Hammond and look around the beach and every spot it could be. I went the other way. I had just gone a few blocks when I spotted it. It was just sitting by the Standard Oil dock. The tide had taken it down there, and all I had to do was jump aboard, start her up, back her out of there, and take it back to our mooring. There wasn't any damage, either to the boat or the dock. But it was sure funny to go down there and find your boat is gone.

～

When we were on vacation in California at Christmas in 1963, the *New Hope* sank in Astoria's East Basin. I got a call that my boat had

New Hope loaded with 150,000 pounds of Pacific Ocean perch, caught in one day off the Oregon Coast.

sunk. I came back right away to Astoria. Only the mast and boom were sticking out of the water. I had left a fellow watching things while I was away. He was to pump the boat out, which he did, but one time he didn't turn the seawater valve all the way off. So the boat filled with water and sank. We raised the boat, and it was a real mess. We checked around the boat to see why it had sunk and found one of the sea valves open. He must have opened it to pump out the boat and forgot to close it. He never did admit it.

I took all the electronics off the boat and soaked everything in fresh water. Then we dried it all out, and all the electronics worked. We did have to overhaul the main engine, but we got everything back to the way it was, although we lay up for a long time.

CHAPTER 7
Not Your Average Family

In 1967, a couple of guys were looking for a place to tie up their boat. It was a minesweeper called the *Tidewater Shaver*. I had a dock over in Young's Bay at Williamsport. I had purchased this dock from a McMindy. So I told them I could rent a place for a 136-foot boat. I charged him $30 a month. They brought it over to the dock and were going to fix this boat up to go tuna fishing. They were in their sixties and they lived on the boat. They had removed the engines for the company that owned the boat, and for payment, the company gave them the boat.

I kept noticing that not much was going on and I knew they would never get it done. It was just too much work for two old fellows. So, finally they asked me if I wanted to buy it. I told them

Kathy Jo before being sold to the Love family from the Queen Anne Hill neighborhood in Seattle.

I'd think about it. It was 136-foot with a 25-foot beam. It didn't have any engines, but it had the propellers, the wiring, and all the steering. All it lacked was propulsion engines, and they only wanted $4,000 for it. There was this guy who drove up in a Cadillac and wore a big Texas hat, looking to buy a boat. So I told him about the boat and then said I would go partners with him if he wanted to buy it. I didn't want to own it alone because I didn't have time. He went down and talked to the old guys about it. He came back and said, "Well, I bought the boat." I said, "I thought we were going to be partners! He said, "Well, you can buy half the boat from me." So I agreed. He asked me what I was going to do with it, so I told him I wanted to put steel over the whole deck so it would never leak. So this guy told me he would send me a whole load of steel. I told him I needed a couple of diesel engines, and he told me he'd send me a couple of engines. I thought to myself that I had a real live one here. He's got steel, he's got engines.

I was getting pretty excited about this deal when the two old guys looked me up. The man's $4,000 check had bounced. We called the bank in Idaho it was drawn on. The man at the bank said, "Oh yeah, this old guy married some gal whose former husband was a house mover and they've got some old army trucks here, some 4 X 4's, and a bunch of junk. He's got a field a few blocks away where he keeps all this stuff. But I don't think the whole doggone junkyard is worth $4,000." Anyway, the check wasn't any good.

I told the two old guys that I didn't really have time to fix the boat, but I'd give them $3,500 for it. And they took it. Then I advertised for a partner and found a guy named Dick Stark. I told him I would furnish all the material if he furnished the labor. We'd put a fish boat together and he could run it. He agreed. I have never seen one guy do so much all by himself. I went down to California and bought a couple of diesel engines and masts and booms and winches. He worked on it for about a year and finally it was ready to go tuna fishing. We went about eighty miles offshore and went jigging. You throw feathered hooks over the stern and those albacore grab them and you haul them in. It takes a lot of time to get fish because you catch them one at a time, but if you stay out long enough, maybe a month at a time, you can catch a lot of tuna and come out pretty well. We did this about three or four years until I wanted to use the boat to go dragging around the Columbia River. I had put two 6-110 General Motors engines in it when I got it, but it really wasn't enough power for a boat that big, so I got a couple of new Cats, 2D 343s, 360-horsepower each, and started dragging with it.

Finally I realized that a boat that big wasn't always good. It took up two hoists when you went to the fish dock. The fish companies hated to see me coming because nobody else would fit at the dock. It was hard to turn and maneuver, especially around docks. So, I got disgusted with it and in 1975 I decided to sell it.

I put an ad in the paper. Some members of a religious cult from Seattle came down to look at it. They looked it over from front to back. One of them said, "It's just what I want. But I can't buy it myself. The family will buy it." I didn't hear from him for a while until he called and said he was bringing a member of the family down. The guy had a leather belt around his waist with a lot of stuff hanging on it. One of the guys was named Serious. He had hair hanging down to his butt and all tied up in a ponytail. I thought to myself "What could this guy buy?" So, I said, "If you're interested in buying the boat, you are going to have to have $48,000 down because I have a mortgage on it from the Production Credit Company in Salem and I have to pay off that mortgage before I sell it to you. Then I'll sell you the boat, carry the mortgage, and hold the paper, and you can pay me for it."

And so we agreed. Then they sent a big school bus of these hippies down. I called them hippies, but it was a religious cult from Queen Anne Hill in Seattle. They were backing a man who was carrying freight from Seattle to Homer, Alaska. Homer is in Cook's Inlet, northeast of Kodiak Island. He would collect maybe $100 from each member to get what they wanted from the Lower 48 and bring it back to them. The cult members were going to crew the boat for him so he wouldn't have to pay any wages for a crew. Cult members didn't work for pay. They worked in exchange for what they needed for life, to accomplish whatever the cult wanted to do.

After I sold them the boat, they wanted me to do some work on the stern. There were a couple of beams that weren't too good, so I told them I would tear out the wood and put in a steel deck with new beams. They would do all the welding and I'd do the layout work and get the thing placed correctly. They agreed so we built a whole new stern. It was about twelve feet by twenty-five feet.

I worked with a big guy, over six feet tall with a full beard. His name was Richness. When a person joined the cult, they all took new names with the last name of Israel. They told me there were over three hundred in the cult, although I never did see that many. They had several houses on Queen Anne Hill. They made their own wine, grew their own gardens, begged extra produce, like the trimmings from the lettuce at grocery stores. They lived very inexpensively. I always suspected they used drugs.

Every time I talked with one of them I would ask them why they joined the cult. Most of them told stories about being down and out with nowhere to go, so they joined the cult. If they had no place to sleep, they had a place at the cult. That's how people came into the cult. They gave all their possessions to the cult when they entered and were not allowed to take anything with them if they left. Richness had given the cult $1.5 million when he entered the cult. It was part of that money they used to buy the boat. They cut themselves off from the world when they came to the cult. They left their things, their old name, their families, and were forbidden to use the phone to make contacts with the outside world. There were a lot of children in the cult. They said all the children belonged to everyone. This was a true commune where there was free love and relationships were very open.

Seven or eight of the cult members lived on the boat while I was working on it. At 5 o'clock in the morning, they'd all leave. They all came together at 5 A.M. for a meeting. It was the only time of the day they could get together since everyone worked in different places at different jobs. So, early in the morning, they all gathered on Queen Anne Hill, had their meeting, and then everyone went to work. Sometimes they worked for the city, mowed lawns, and took care of all their gardening. They were always trading work for something. They also got donations from the public, and whatever cult members brought with them when they entered the family.

One time the cult invited my wife, June, and I up to the cult headquarters for dinner. They had special steaks for us, but the rest of the cult members didn't get too much. When they came in with the food, they always bowed down to the Love Israel, the cult leader. He was like a god to those people, the way they treated him.

We didn't have a shower on the boat, so they asked if I wanted to come up to the house and take a shower. So I went up there, and they didn't have a shower there either. They only had a tub, and there was a board across the tub with a Bible on it. I had to take the board and the Bible and put it aside so I could take a bath.

Once when we were working on the stern, I went to Astoria for about a week to spend time with my family. When I came back, these guys had taken a chain saw and cut the bulwarks off both sides of the boat. They said they wanted to make the house wider, all the way out to the side of the boat. There was about three feet of deck between the house and the rail. It was covered by the deck above, so you could walk along there without getting wet. I told them, "You can't do that! Don't you know this boat has now the maximum size house it can have without hiring a licensed engineer and skipper? If you get it any bigger than it is, you're going to have to hire a licensed skipper and have the boat remeasured!" They didn't know that. They just cut it off and thought they could do anything they wanted. So they had to build it all back again. They had to go under the deck and put new frames in the side, and it was a big job. They hired a guy from Astoria I knew to do it. His name was Roy Atwood. He used to work for the Navy and was a really good shipwright. He could put in planks or anything, a real clever guy. He wanted to go hunting in Alaska and they were going to be the guide for him up there hunting in Homer. So, he agreed to do this work on the boat in exchange for the hunting trip. I don't know if he ever got his hunting trip. He had cancer. I think he went to Portland and, the last time I heard, he had passed away. And that's the way it goes.

One time we were on the boat and we ran out of fuel, so we couldn't even keep the generators running. They said they couldn't go and get any because they had no money at all. "The Lord will provide," they said. And, sure enough, a day or so later, there came a couple of barrels of fuel. We got the generators running again and we were back in business.

One of the members was named Logic. He was the son of Steve Allen, the comedian songwriter. Love Israel's real name was Paul Erdman and he was from the Clatskanie, Oregon, area. Another was Courage. He was to be the skipper of the boat although he really didn't know very much about it. I was to teach him. So I came on board and I told him if he was going to learn how to run this boat, he was going to have to take the bull by the horns and do it. I told him he'd never learn if I came on board and moved the boat around and did everything for him. We were going fishing the next day so I told him to take the boat by himself up to Bumble Bee Cold Storage and get ice for the trip and then come back and tie it up to the dock. It would be good experience for him. So, off he went.

In a little while he came back and his chin was dropped and I saw him walking away from the boat. I said, "What's wrong?" And he said, "I hit a rock! I didn't know there was a buoy over there by the Bumble Bee Cold Storage with a can on it to indicate the sunken rock. So I backed up the boat and hit the rock." He didn't know how much damage he had done. But I told him, "Boy, now you're in real trouble. We can't go on dry dock here in Astoria because the yard is full of boats and we'll have to take it all the way to Portland and that is a hundred miles away. But I'll tell you what you could do. I don't know how bad the propellers are bent, but I got a wrench here that will fit the nuts that hold the propellers on. You've got divers aboard. You could send a guy down there and put that wrench on the nut. Then we'll put a big eight-foot pipe over the handle of the wrench. Then we can hook the pipe to the chain block and pull the nut loose. Maybe we can get those propellers off and look at them. So if you want to send a guy down there and take a look at it and see if the wheels are bent and what's happening, I'll tell you what to do. And if you go down there and get the nuts loose and back them off about one inch, then we could start the engine up and get a few revolutions going on it pretty fast and then all of a sudden we'll put it in reverse and maybe that pressure on the wheel might take the wheel off the taper, and we won't lose the wheel. It will hit that nut an inch away and it will be loose and easy to get the wheel off."

We did get the wheels fixed up and they did this job in the water. They never had to haul the boat out or anything. It really surprised me that they did get those off that way. I had never done that before, but it sure worked out good. I knew the propellers were on there tight. Normally you had to heat them with a torch and hit them with a sledgehammer and a lot of other things, but I had never tried it with putting the engine in reverse. With the engine running at high speed, there was quite a bit of torque there. By golly, when the diver went down, he did it just like I said, and it pulled them right off. He got the nuts loose on the propellers and he got the propellers loose like I told him. They brought the wheels up on the deck and, sure enough, they were bent. But now we could take them to the machine shop and get them straightened out and back in ship shape again. So I said, "Now there's another thing. After you get those wheels off, you might have a bent shaft. If that propeller hit a rock, you could have bent the shaft. I'll tell you what you do. You send this diver back down there and take any kind of a one-foot rule. Go down and hold this rule against the shaft and stern post, and we'll start the engine and run the shaft. Now if that rule doesn't go in and out, but stays the same when it turns, then you don't have a bent shaft. But if it goes in and out, any movement at all, then you got a bent shaft. Then you're in real trouble." So, we did it, started the engine up but none of the shafts were bent. They were back in business without going to Portland or on dry dock.

Courage was running the boat in Alaska and got caught in a hundred–mile-per-hour wind. It was very rough and they almost lost the boat, but they got to shore and into some shelter. Then they were dragging out of Anacortes for a while to get enough fish to feed the family. But the skipper got tired of fishing. Fishing is pretty lonely and isolated. He must have missed the company of the family and the women of the cult.

They decided to sell the boat to the guy they bought it for in the first place. They sold it for $20,000 down and $20,000 a month. This guy was going to fish herring roe above Bristol Bay. The Japanese were paying a big price for herring roe. So he went up there but there wasn't any herring. Then he got a chance to tow a barge above Goodnews Bay to Kodiak Island. It was more than a thousand miles. The skipper had his brother as engineer and his son as a deck hand, and some other kids as deck hands.

They were getting ready to tow the barge and got the big towlines wound up in the propellers and wound so tightly it choked both engines. Then I got word in Astoria that the boat had burned up—that they burned it on purpose to collect the insurance. The skipper told his brother that he could put in an extra $5,000 claim to the insurance for his tools that he lost in the fire. But the brother was a religious man and couldn't lie about it, so he went to Seattle and told the state patrol that they had burned the boat on purpose. That started a real argument between the two brothers. The skipper said his brother was crazy and the brother maintained his story about burning the boat. It really backfired on them, however, because they discovered that their insurance didn't cover them in that

Love family members with George in August 1975 on board *Kathy Jo*.

area. There was a limitation on the policy that determined certain boundaries for coverage. So the insurance company refused to pay.

I was pretty concerned about this because I still had the mortgage on the boat. The cult had wanted to cancel the insurance on the boat because it was costing them $15,000 a year. I told them that if they didn't want to carry insurance I would have to take the boat back. If they would give me a mortgage on a piece of property they owned, then they wouldn't have to carry insurance on the boat, as long as my interest in the boat was covered. So they gave me a mortgage on 140 acres they had on the Kenai Peninsula near Homer. I kept that for a while and then they wanted to sell it. So they gave me a mortgage on a piece of property they owned in Hawaii. Then they wanted to sell that. So they said they would give me a mortgage on 140 acres near Burlington, Washington. They had a whole mountainside there, with a lake and a half million dollars worth of timber on it. That was when the boat burned in Alaska.

The insurance company, for some reason, paid me off. There was a clause in the policy that said they could make one round trip to Alaska. I think the only reason they paid me off was they wanted to prosecute the guys who burned their own boat. It isn't against the law to burn your own boat, but if you try to fraudulently collect insurance money, it is a crime. So, I got my money, and then later the family wanted me to release my interest in the mountain property, since I was paid off. It was quite a deal, and a big ordeal, but it was an interesting time dealing with the cult.

I haven't seen them or been there recently. I heard Love Israel, the leader, left the cult for a year or two but then came back. I think the family is still in existence over in Burlington where they live in tents and grow their own food. Maybe I'll run into them some day. I don't know.

I heard when the cult broke up on Queen Anne Hill that Richness, the guy with the million and a half, got most of the property. It was his money they had used for it.

I can't help but think, after my experience with them, that if a son or daughter is missing, they well might belong to a cult like this, but they are so hard to find because they change their names, their identity, and live a totally different life. Young people can hide in a place like this, and a lot of them do. They want somebody to tell them what to do. They don't want to take responsibility for themselves.

CHAPTER 8
Keeping Them All Afloat

I had just come in from a three- to four-day trip on the *Coolidge II*. I had tied up to the dock but didn't unload as I had to go to Portland on business. I asked my engineer to take the boat from the basin up to the fish house to unload. We were gone all day. About six the next morning I got a marine call from Al Mather on the *Trask* who told me the boat was sitting pretty low in the bow. So, I jumped in the car and raced down there and, sure enough, there was water over the top of the engine and she was going down. I called the fire department and they came with their big suction hoses and pumped her out. In the meantime I called my engineer and asked him if he turned off the valves. He said he didn't remember, so we went down there. There are two valves on one side of the engine. When

Coolidge II nearly sunk.

you pump out a boat you open those valves to prime the pump. Then after the pump has its prime, you turn the sea cock off and the pumps empty the bilge. Evidently he forgot to turn them off and the boat filled with water.

The engineer didn't want to admit what had happened. He didn't want the black mark on his record as an engineer so he never did admit it. But when he got there he waded down into the engine room. I would never have done that because when water gets in the boat it is really greasy and you get it all over yourself. But he waded down there. I think he went and closed the valves with his foot, because when they pumped it out, the valves were shut. But, in order to save face, he just didn't admit anything. But we got it pumped out and flushed the engine out, and everything was okay.

⌒

When we had the *Elector* we were tied up to a dock in the river and a big westerly wind came up. The boat broke loose. About three in the morning a guy came to my house. "Hey, your boat broke loose and it's under the dock up at Bumble Bee Cold Storage." So I jumped in the car and went down there and, sure enough, there it was under the dock in a big swell. About three or four feet of the stern was jammed in there. It must have been blowing fifty miles an hour with big breakers in the river. Every time the boat came up on a swell, it would lift the dock up. There was also a big transformer right there where the boat was. A guy who was there told me not to move the boat or I would knock out the transformer. The Coast Guard was also there, but they couldn't get near the boat. But I was worried about my boat. So when it came up on a swell I jumped down on the boat and started her up and got her out of there. Boy, I was taking breakers and spray was going all over the boat, but I got her out of there. We were lucky.

⌒

Once when we were on the *Muzon* and we were at the mouth of the Columbia River, we had a big load of dogfish on board. The pipe the rudder shaft goes through came loose, and water was leaking in the stern. It was coming in so fast I thought for sure we were going to lose the boat. But we just kept running, and we got in just in time.

I bought the *Rodoma* in 1956 from the Pacific American Fisheries for $3,500. They were selling all their old fish tenders. It was one of the best ones they had. The engine was shot but the hull was good. I rigged it up for dragging in Astoria. Then I needed a skipper because I was busy with the *New Hope*. So I had hired a guy named Tony Stanovich to fish with me for a while. I liked him and so I asked him if he wanted to run a boat. He liked the idea so he ran the *Rodoma* for a month or so.

One day I went down to the boat and there was Tony, climbing a rope up to the top of the boom, hand over hand. He got all the way up to the top and yelled down, "Hey, my muscles are frozen and I can't get down." I told him that was too bad. He got himself up there and nobody else was going to go up and get him down. So he finally came down.

After he had been running the boat for a month or so, I went down to the *Rodoma* asking for Tony. There was another guy on the boat but Tony wasn't there. I asked him, "Where's Tony?" "Oh!" he

Muzon loaded.

said, "He hired me to run the boat for him, and I canned him!" I said, "How could you do that? He was in charge!" "Well," he said, "I may not have been able to can him, but I did!"

In 1968 I sold the *Rodoma* to a couple of guys. They gave me $6,000 down. I held the mortgage for the balance. One of them wanted to do the bookkeeping himself to save money, but it was a big mistake to let him do it. He never paid the bills nor the insurance premium. We heard over the radio that the *Rodoma* sank in just a few minutes after hitting a submerged object. The skipper was alone on the boat on a run from Newport to Astoria. It was foggy. He got on a life raft and drifted for twenty-four hours before he was rescued. I never did believe his story and actually think he sank the boat deliberately. I never did get the balance of my money.

I saw him a few years later at Westport. He was on drugs. He had lost his wife and two children as a result of his drug habit. But I lost a lot, too. I had $30,000 coming from that deal. This turned out to be my biggest loss while I was in the fishing business.

In 1965 we were fishing on the *Mary R.* We were anchored in the river by Cape Disappointment off Waikiki Beach, sorting fish. We wanted to take advantage of a good flood tide so we could get back to Astoria a little faster. I was at the wheel, steering for the buoy light at the end of the jetty near Ilwaco. The side window was open while we were running. All of a sudden I heard a lot of birds and realized we must be pretty close to the shore. I turned the wheel hard over, but we hit the rocks at the end of the jetty. The tide was flooding so fast that we were being pushed sideways, sending us off course enough to hit the rocks. The boat started to sink immediately, so one of the crew, Mike Searls, volunteered to swim to the jetty. We tied a rope around his waist so if he missed the end of the jetty by the force of the tide, we could pull him back. But he was a strong swimmer and he made it. Then each of the crew jumped in the water, holding onto the rope that he secured on the jetty, and everybody made it to shore before the boat sank.

⤶

I always had a place to store my fishing gear. I bought a warehouse on Young's Bay that had a dock where I could tie my boat and do all my repairs. The *Eagle* hit a rock and broke the bow stem. It was dry docked at the Astoria Marine Construction Company. They had some trouble with the new Cat engine that was in the boat. Don Fastabend was the boss at the shipyard. They were having trouble with the insurance company as well as the Caterpillar people. The Cat people took the engine back while the *Eagle* was still on dry dock. Then the yard caught on fire and burned the bow half of the boat so it laid on dry dock for a long time. Finally they wanted the boat off the dry dock to continue their shipyard business. The owner had to move the boat off the ways and wanted to rent dock space from me. I agreed. The Eagle was patched up with canvas for the move to my dock. The owner, Gene Nadon, had to come down twice a week to pump it out so it wouldn't sink at the dock. This went on for some time. One day I asked Gene if I could buy the boat. He sold it for $8,500.

It was a big job to rebuild it. I had a ramp where I could beach the boat at my warehouse, so I pulled it up on the beach, bow first. It was there for months before I got it replanked, a new stem put in and a new engine installed. Finally I got it done and started dragging with it. This was an 87-foot halibut schooner. It was old but it was in good shape.

A fellow from California was looking for a schooner to buy for dragging out of Bodega Bay, just north of San Francisco. He gave me $10,000 down and $50,000 on contract, promising me 15 percent of the catch for payments on the fifty thousand. Boy, did he ever do well with that boat. I got big checks from fish sales and he paid me off.

~

I saw in the Astoria paper an ad to sell the shrimper *Tide*. When I checked into it, I found out a woman was selling the boat, but the boat was in her husband's name. She said her husband was sleeping in his truck and she couldn't find him to make the deal. Finally he came to the house and we finished the deal, but it took about two weeks.

~

I got a fellow to run the *Tide* for shrimp for about a year. It didn't turn out very well, so I decided to sell one-half interest to a fellow by the name of Bill Page, an experienced shrimp skipper from the Texas gulf area. The engine on the boat was nearly worn out. A sport boat had run on the beach near the *Peter Iredale*, so I bought the engine and put it, a D 343 Cat diesel, in the *Tide*.

We just got a good start fishing for crab and shrimp in 1982. Bill was running the *Tide*. He was fishing off Leadbetter Point. About midnight, Bill went down to get a little sleep and a crew member took the wheel while they were running back to Astoria. The guy got his lights mixed up. He started going into the Willapa Bay instead of the Columbia River. He hit bottom and called mayday. A copter came out and took the crew off the boat. The *Tide* turned over in the water and disappeared.

⤵

A little tugboat, *Arrow IV*, went up for bid by an insurance company. It was a 46-footer with a double house on it, and a 6-110 Jimmy in it. It had sunk, but now it was on the beach at Oregon City, up the Willamette near Portland. They had lifted it up with a crane. It looked like it was in pretty good shape and I wouldn't have to do very much to it, so I put in a $2,600 bid on it. I figured for that price I would do well. I got the bid, went down and started it up, cleaned it up a bit and brought it down to Astoria and tied it up at the boat basin. I'd go look at it once in a while. One day a real estate friend of mine asked me where my tug was. I told him it was right where it always was, tied up to the dock, but he said he had just come from there and didn't see it.

I dashed down there, and he was right, it wasn't there. I couldn't figure out what could happen to a 46-foot tug. So I started looking around and called the Coast Guard to see if they had seen it drifting down the river, going over the bar or something. But nobody knew anything about it.

The next day I went back to the basin and I saw a light about six inches below the water. It wasn't burning, but it looked like a mast light. Sure enough, that was my tug. It got caught under the dock when the tide came up and it just filled full of water. I had to get some cranes together and raise it. It was really heavy. I didn't realize it before I bought it, but this boat was made out of solid teakwood. I met a guy who had worked on the boat and knew they had taken the teak off an old battleship across the river in Ilwaco years ago and built this tug out of it. All the decks, planks, and the house were teak. But teak is very heavy. We sent down a diver who put a strap around it, and the cranes lifted her up.

After we got the tug fixed up again, I put an ad in the paper and sold it to a guy from Blaine. He took it there and turned it into a one-man dragger. He would go out for the day and then come in each night and unload. They put everything in a little brailer and left it on deck. Then they dropped it into the buggy, weighed it up and sold it. He could do all this in about ten minutes. Then he'd tie the boat up, and go home, and start all over the next day. It was truly a one-man operation. However, soon after he bought it, he got cancer and passed away. I see the boat is still up there. I think it was handed down to his son.

CHAPTER 9
Recycling Before Its Time

I bought a lot of surplus stuff. It was kind of a hobby for me. I loved the challenge of buying something and rebuilding it or fixing it up and selling it. When I wasn't doing anything else I could do this, so I would always have something to do and make jobs for myself while I wasn't fishing.

⤳

In 1964 there was a 65-foot, 18-foot beam wood Coast Guard boat up for bid in Camden, New Jersey. I was in Astoria so I hired a photographer near Camden to take lots of pictures of the boat, inside and out, and send them to me. It looked good in the pictures so I bid $4,500 on it. I won the bid, so I went back there to see what I bought. It had a six-cylinder Murphey diesel in good shape. I moved the boat from the Coast Guard station to a shipyard near Cape May, New Jersey, and put it on dry dock, where I checked the bottom of the boat and fixed everything that was needed. Then I launched it, tied it up to a float and returned to Astoria.

I advertised for a partner and found one who agreed to go out there and bring it back to Astoria. The deal was that he would bring the boat at his expense in exchange for one-third interest in the boat. He took the vessel from Cape May but only got as far as Fernandina Beach, Florida. He was having problems maintaining oil pressure. I drove back there, and I found the problem, but decided not to go any further. So I put the boat up for sale and, within a few months, had it sold. I lost money on it, but I got a chance to see the East Coast and Atlantic City, so it was worth it.

⤳

I was also interested in auctions. I bought the minesweeper that way. I also bid on a dozen ship booms near Oakland, California, a ship galley range, and a Navy woodworking unit. That was just what I needed to convert the minesweeper into a dragger.

↪

Once I bid on a 78-foot dragger that had been in a collision. The stem was damaged. The insurance company was looking for bids. I was the high bidder but the owner decided to keep the vessel, so I lost out on that one.

↪

I bid on a five-bedroom house in Warrenton and got it. I rebuilt it so it looked like new. I then sold it and came out good on it.

↪

I bid on a garage in Bellingham, built by the Voc Tech School. They wanted $4,200 as a starting bid. I told them I would bid $3,500 if it didn't sell. After the bidding was over they called me and said it was mine. I cut the garage in half, put it on a boat trailer, separated the two halves, added twenty-five feet in between and made a nice house out of it.

↪

In 1985 the *Angela Carol* came up for bid by the Production Credit Association. I bid along with a friend of mine and got it for $95,000. Thirty days later, after overhauling the engine, we sold it for $24,000 profit.

↪

In 1957 after fishing shrimp for a Westport shrimp cannery, I decided to get into the shrimp canning business. Joe Anderson had a small custom salmon cannery for sport fishermen located in an old leased plant that would be ideal for shrimp. It was in Warrenton, Oregon. I talked Joe into it and we began the Pacific Shrimp, Incorporated. I was the president, Bud Conger Jr. was the secretary, and Joe was the manager. It was tough getting started because it was hard to sell canned shrimp. Draggers made more money dragging than they did shrimping, so it was hard to get boats to fish shrimp.

But we were in the business twenty-two years before we sold out to some guys. They bought it on contract but went broke, so we lost two-thirds of our money.

I was fishing with the *New Hope* during the cannery years and salvaging boats on the side. A cannery tender came down from Portland, going to Puget Sound. He got into problems and went ashore on Peacock Spit. The owner heard I bought salvaged boats and looked me up and told me he would sell me the boat for $350. I got my tools and went out there and salvaged the engine out of this 65-foot cannery tender. The next day it broke up in the surf.

∼

There was another 70-foot boat that went on the beach by the partially submerged sailing vessel *Peter Iredale*. I salvaged the bow anchor winch. When the insurance company heard this, they called me and asked for it back. I told them I would give them the anchor winch if they would pay me for my time to get it. I wanted $300 for the winch or I would give them $50 for the title to it. They took the $50. It was a good deal because a new winch would have cost $1,500. I put it on the *Georgene M.,* which didn't have one.

CHAPTER 10
Taking Bottom Fishing Too Literally

We did a lot of our dragging off the Columbia River because it was good fishing, and I didn't have to run very far to get our net in the water and on the bottom. One time I saw a friend of mine, Jack Stanovich, on the *Silverland*. He was waving to me, so I came up alongside. He told me his gear was hung up on the bottom and he had been there all day trying to get free. His cables were so tight they were ready to break. He was about ready to cut the cables and go home, but I thought I would try something first. We took a big shackle and the end of my cable, hooked it around his, and dropped it down to the bottom. I started towing the opposite direction to the way he was going when he got stuck, and, by golly, it came loose. We got all his gear back. This was a big deal because a loss like that would have been thousands of dollars, even in those days. He went back to fishing and was one happy man. We saved the day for him.

〜

I was on the Columbia, making a tow across the river mouth, and I had a whole deck load of female crabs. We were throwing them overboard, trying to clean up the deck. Veiko Romppanen was on the *Valhalla II*, fishing right outside of me. He started to pick up his net and was telling another fisherman on the radio that there was something awfully heavy in it. He said he was going to try to tow it to the beach. Usually when we got a big rock or something in the net, we'd try to get it into shallow water so we could get our doors back and pick up the net with the boom. I got on the radio and told him that he had crabs. He came right back and said "If these are crabs, I'll eat them." We didn't hear any more from him the rest of the day. The next morning we called him, "What did you have in the net yesterday?" He came back, "Well, I guess I got to eat them, because I had crabs." Sometimes those crabs come in and they're really thick and all females. He had a whole bag full of them so they were really heavy.

⌐

One time I was dragging near the mouth of the river with the *Georgene M.* I got the net stuck on the bottom and couldn't get it back. So we just stuck a buoy on the end of it and left it there. We went back to town to get a diver. He went down and found it was a really big anchor. So we hooked our double block to it and lifted it up. The anchor was about twelve feet long and had about sixty feet of chain attached to it. The links on the chain were about half an inch in diameter. One link would have weighed twenty pounds. It was all rusty and just a huge thing. It had been down there many, many years, no doubt from one of those early sailing schooners. I gave the anchor to the diver for his work. I thought about giving it to the maritime museum, but I gave it to the diver so I wouldn't owe him anything.

⌐

After the war there were a lot of things that came floating in by the mouth of the Columbia. We used to get a lot of glass balls wrapped in netting. They were tied on the Japanese fishermen's nets and would break loose. Some of them were as big as twelve to fourteen inches in diameter although most of them were around six inches.

One time we came out to the mouth of the river and saw a mine floating in the water not too far from No. 2 Buoy near the ship channel. This thing must have been three feet in diameter with a lot of horns sticking out. It was all green and must have been floating around ever since World War II. It either floated a long way, or it may have been dropped here to impede our shipping. All I know is, if we had hit it, it would have been all over for us or any other boat or ship that hit it. It was really a dangerous thing to be floating around, so we called the Coast Guard. They told us to stand by and they would come out and take care of it. We had to stay there until they arrived. When they got there, we left and went to the fishing grounds. I don't know what the Coast Guard did with it, whether they shot at it right there and exploded it, or if they somehow took it in.

Lloyd Sandness and George Moskovita with sailing ship anchor in 1949.

⌁

We used to get depth charges out in deep water when we were drag-ging. They were about eighteen inches in diameter and maybe three feet long. It took two guys just to lift one of them. We didn't call the Coast Guard for those. We just took them out in deeper water, maybe three hundred fathom, and dropped them overboard. We'd put it on the rail, and when the boat rolled, we'd push it over, and then we'd all holler "Bang!" in case it did go off, but it never did. I understand the planes had to unload their explosives before they came in because if they landed with a depth charge, it might be dan-gerous. I don't know if these came from planes, subs, or destroyers. When you scoop up everything on the bottom of the ocean, you just never know what you're going to get. You get old bottles in addition to all sorts of fish. We always brought in the things we caught and looked them over. It is just one of the things that makes the fishing business so interesting.

⌁

One time we got a skull in the net. We brought it in and called the Coast Guard. I told them to let me know when they found out who it was. I guess they never did. A guy could have fallen off a ship or who knows what in all the years that skull had been down there.

It was the first time I ever got one of those. I did take some pictures of it.

↫

On the *New Zealand* we started picking up the bag and we couldn't do it. We put several turns on the gypsy head, but it wouldn't come. I thought maybe we were hooked on a nail sticking out of the boat, so I put a couple more turns on the gypsy head and finally it came up. There was a big octopus in the cod end with one of his legs sticking out through a hole in the net. Evidently the leg had been attached to the hull with its suction cups and was holding pretty tight until we put the extra pressure on with a double block.

Sure enough, there was a great big devil fish when we dumped the bag. You can sell an octopus to the Japanese for a good price, so it was worth bringing in.

↫

I never will forget the time we got a bomb in our nets. We were dragging with the *Kathy Jo* off the Washington Coast. One of the crew I had said, "You gotta call the Coast Guard. Man, one of my buddies got killed with one of these things. You gotta call the Coast Guard." I was just going to dump it back over again. I didn't want to monkey with it as I was pretty sure if I called the Coast Guard, we'd have to stop fishing and run the bomb back into port or something. But he insisted I call the Coast Guard. So I called and gave them our position, about four hours off the Washington Coast. Then he said, "Get off your boat!" And I said, "Onto what?" We didn't even have a lifeboat aboard. We did have a raft but we weren't about to get off our boat. There wasn't anything wrong with the boat, and I told him I wasn't scared of this thing. We had it hanging in the rigging and it was still in the fish bag. When the boat rolled, the bag would hit the rail and the boat would roll the other way and it would hit the hatch, but we weren't afraid because the bomb was cushioned by a lot of fish all around it.

He told us to bring it in but not to anchor in the ship channel. They said for a dangerous item like this they would send down some demolition experts from Port Angeles in a plane. So we went in and anchored off Sand Island, just off the channel. About two in the morning these fellows came alongside from the Coast Guard station at Ilwaco. They came on board and said, "Don't touch the bomb. Don't touch anything." So they got out their books and started looking for serial numbers. I told them to go ahead and do what they needed to do while we went in the house for some coffee. They finally came into the galley and asked if we could help them. They couldn't get it out of the net. So we got it out for them. They scratched around on it and found a lot of numbers on it. Finally they determined it was a drill bomb. It was a phony. It wasn't even a real bomb. It was the same shape and everything, but it was a practice bomb. I asked them what they were going to do with it. They said we couldn't dump it in the river because the gillnetters would catch it. I told them I would take it to town. We took it up to the mooring basin and put it on the dock. The media was there and took pictures of it, and a big article was written up about it.

You lose a lot of fishing time with things like that. We didn't usually call the Coast Guard because it just took time. We couldn't waste the time. We had to go fishing. If we called the Coast Guard every time, we'd never make a trip.

The bomb lay there on the dock in the basin. It must have been there several months, and all of a sudden somebody came down and noticed the bomb and called the Coast Guard. They came down and investigated again. I guess they didn't know how it got there. They put it in a truck and took it out to Camp Rilea. I said, "Hey, what are you going to do with that bomb? That's my bomb. I want my bomb back!" So there was another article in the paper. This one had headlines: "Moskovita wants his bomb back." I thought about going out there and getting my bomb, bringing it back home for a souvenir, but I didn't.

CHAPTER 11

He Was a Character, That Guy

We were on the *Kathy Jo* and were going out fishing about midnight. I had to run down to the warehouse and get an extra net. I yelled to the cook to come with me. He got on the rail and got a hold of the dock sheet piling. What I didn't know was that the guy was drunk. He tried to get up on the dock. There was no ladder at that spot and he couldn't do it. He just hung there. There was another guy on the boat and we both tried to get him up on the dock, but he weighed about three hundred pounds. He was hanging between the boat and the dock. Finally we got his hands up on the second rail. I held him there and wasn't going to let him go because if I dropped him, he'd drown. There wasn't much room between the boat and the dock. I figured I had him now unless his arms broke off.

It was about midnight by now when we were supposed to leave for fishing and we still hadn't gotten our net, so I hollered as loud as I could, "Help! Help! Man overboard! *Kathy Jo*." Everybody knew the boat because we had been fishing here for some time. I hollered constantly for about fifteen or twenty minutes as loud as I could. And, by golly, the *Jenny Decker* was just leaving to go out fishing at that time and he happened to hear me holler. He tied up alongside our boat and with his help we got him up on the dock. But he was really in pain. We called 911 and had the ambulance come down and pick him up to take him to the hospital. I thought maybe his arms were out of joint because he was so heavy. They got him on a stretcher and took him to the hospital. He was hospitalized for a while, but he was okay. It was a tough deal but we made it. I was just glad I could hold him until I got help, and it was sure lucky the *Jenny Decker* came by.

～

One time a friend and I were putting in some new pilings under my dock next to Sebastian Stuart Fish Company. The pilings get worn out with the tide constantly going up and down. They are creosoted and last about fifty years, but my dock was about that old, so they were wearing out, one by one. Whenever the tide was right and we had some time, we would change one. When they looked like an hourglass, we'd kick out the old one and put in a new one. There was this guy helping us named Tiny, who was a really big guy. He wasn't too smart, but he weighed about three hundred pounds. We had to jack up the building while we replaced the piling. I told him to be sure to have the jack straight up and down and not slanted in any way. If it was slanted, it could easily jackknife. I left him there while he was jacking up the building, and wouldn't you know it, it jackknifed, and this big guy went overboard. We had to do this job at low tide so we could walk underneath on a plank in between the pilings. I yelled for him to hang on to the piling while I went to find a ladder. Since he was so big, I knew I couldn't lift him out of the river. We had ladders in the warehouse, but it took me about fifteen minutes to get one. I got back as soon as I could, but I was really worried he would drown before I got back. But I got the ladder down to him and he got out okay.

～

When I first started rebuilding the *Jo Ann* (originally the *Aurora*), I hired a guy to work with me. The engine had been underwater for a couple of weeks and I wanted to find out if it was any good. I wanted to start it up, but the rocker arms of the main engine were frozen. So I told him to hit them with a hammer, use a little oil if he needed to and get them moving. Then we would pump some air to see if it would operate (this engine uses air to start). I took off for Long Beach to get some material for the boat. When you're rebuilding a boat, it takes a lot of pipe and this and that, so I was always running around to junkyards to see what I could find.

I was gone for a day, came back, and he had taken those rocker arms and polished them like a new penny. They were really clean. I said to him, "My gosh! Here you got these all off and all cleaned up, but you might just have done all this work for nothing. If it runs, you've done a good thing because it is all ready to paint. But, we just might have to haul this engine off to the junkyard if it won't run!" But the engine started, so we saved it.

Then I told him, "I have two carpenters working on the boat. You do whatever they want you to do to help them out. Those two guys are expensive, and you don't make half what one of them makes, so if there's something they're doing that you could do, you do it and let them do the hard stuff. That's why we have you here." This went on for several days and then he stopped me and said, "You know something? You give me a lot of jobs to do on the boat, but you never let me finish any of them. Just when I get started, you take me off the job and let those other guys finish it." So I told him, "That's exactly the way I want it. The carpenters will do the finish work, but if there is any tearing out to do, I want you to do that. You do the things that don't take much experience, and let them do the work I'm paying them to do. So, you do whatever they tell you, and that's why you are here."

He got disgusted at this, but I told him to stick around, do what he could, work on his own, and I wouldn't rush him. So he stayed. He drank too much and he missed several years of his life because of it. Finally he quit that and things went pretty well for him. He taught himself to weld and got pretty good at it. In the evenings he would invite his buddies to come down to the boat and he would show them what he had done that day.

When he was helping me in California, he married a Mexican gal. I got him a job on one of the tuna boats. When I saw him, he was complaining that the other crew members didn't work hard enough. I told him not to worry about the other guy. It might be the skipper's brother or something. But he couldn't let it go. Finally he quit, it bothered him so much. I saw him one day in one of the bars in San Pedro. He was trying to sell a fifty-dollar watch for ten bucks to buy a couple of drinks. After he had quit for so many years, he went back to it. I heard he died about seven or eight years ago.

⁓

There are a lot of albatross that come around the boat when we're offshore. Harlan Niemi, one of my crew members, made a flat piece of tin and cut a little hole in the middle about half an inch wide.

He put some cheese in the triangle, tied a string on it, and threw it overboard. These *goony birds,* as albatross are called, would grab the cheese and then get their beak caught in that little hole in the center. We'd catch them and bring them aboard. He got a kick out of it and got a lot of them on the deck. But, once they were there, they couldn't fly off the boat unless we picked them up and threw them off. They didn't have enough room on the boat to get started. It was one of the things he did while we were dragging and there was nothing else to do.

Another time while Harlan was fishing with us we were tied up to a cannery dock in Coos Bay. He went up and got drunk one night. On the way back to the boat, he grabbed a cart used to bring freight down to the boats on the dock. It weighed about sixty pounds but he threw it down on top of the *Elector* and broke the skylight. This was about two in the morning. The crew came running out of that boat like a bunch of rats, as they slept right underneath the skylight. He sure did a lot of damage in a hurry. We had to get it fixed before going out again.

When we had the *Kathy Jo,* I let one of the crew members sleep on the boat as he didn't have any place to stay. The phone rang at 2:30 in the morning saying he had a fire on the boat he couldn't cope with. I went right down and everything was ablaze. He called the fire department but they couldn't get to the boat. It was tied up at the upper basin in Astoria. The dock there was not very sturdy, so they didn't dare bring the fire engines out there. So they hooked up to water a couple blocks away and had to drag their hoses all the way down to the boat. This crew member knew how to start the engine, so he got it started and hooked up our own hose and pretty well put out the fire before the firemen got down there. But it burned pretty badly. We ended up having to redo the whole galley and were laid up for three to four months before we got it back into shape.

That's what you get when you do a person a favor. He would go out drinking at night, and come back drunk after the bars closed. So, just by being nice to this guy and giving him a place to sleep, he put us out of a job for a while.

∽

Another time I hired a man to go fishing with us. Just before we left he said he didn't have any boots, so I gave him some money to buy some boots. We got all ready to go again and he said his wife didn't have anything to eat. He said he couldn't go out fishing and leave her there with nothing to eat. So I gave him $50 as an advance on his share, to keep his wife from starving.

∽

One time we were getting ready to go fishing with the *Rodoma* and we were tied up at the foot of Twelfth Street in Astoria. I invited this crew member to come with me to town and get a sandwich. Before we left, I told him to turn off the diesel stove. I didn't see any need to let it burn when we weren't there. When we came back after eating, there was a fire engine down by the boat, and they were chopping holes in the deck with their axes and tearing up the boat. The guy had turned the valve on the stove the wrong way and instead of turning it off, he opened it up wide. So we had a fire in the galley and it also burned the stateroom. We lost a week of fishing there. It's really hard to rely on someone else to do something for you.

∽

We had a procedure when we were dragging with the *Kathy Jo*. After we lifted the net, we picked it up with the boom, and then backed the boat up to get the net alongside the boat. One time I told the crew member to watch the net and if the net started to get under the boat toward the wheel, to holler. The pilothouse is a long way from the net and I couldn't see the back of the boat. So I yelled back to ask him if it was all clear because I was ready to back up. He said it was, but it wasn't. We backed right over the net and got it caught in the wheel. It was a twin screw engine, but I didn't dare use the other screw because we might get the net caught in both of them. We called the Coast Guard and they came out with their boat, the *Yacona*, and towed us back to Astoria. We had to go on dry dock, and that's expensive. It was wound up real bad. I don't think a diver could have gotten it loose. Those kinds of things are always a danger when you're fishing. You almost have to look yourself unless you have somebody who knows what they are looking for. It doesn't take much of a mistake to get in trouble. That's what you go through when you're running a boat as a fisherman.

⤚

We had a fellow, Mike Mitchell, an American Indian, who could see fish jump when no one else could. His eyes would go back and forth across the water, and he'd see the fish break the water. None of us had to see it if Mike had seen it. We'd go right ahead and lay the net out. And we'd always get fish.

Now Mike used to drink a lot. Sometimes he would come aboard the boat drunk, and when we were running out to go fishing, he would be in his bunk with a hangover. I remember him putting his hand up to his throat and would yell, "Let go, let go there, let go, let go!" He was visualizing snakes choking him. We'd have a bottle of whiskey handy and give him a little bit at a time to keep him from going into withdrawal.

He was such a good crew member with the net, and sighting the fish, we needed him and tended to overlook his drinking problem. He would sober up when we were out fishing.

⤚

I lost my best cook and shipmaster, Rocco Danielovich, when he fell off his gillnet boat near Tongue Point. They found his body on the beach near Westport, Washington several days later. He was fishing with me on the *Elector* when I took that big break on the Columbia River bar. He was also fishing with me when I first started dragging in Astoria and he fished with me for many years before he drowned. He was a real chef. He used to cook sea cucumbers, porpoise, and a lot of other seafoods. He made the best pork spareribs and cabbage. I never had any better than his.

⤚

Jackie Ray was a young man twenty years old that came from the East Coast. He wanted to go out with us and learn the fishing business. We didn't really want to take him, but he insisted. We only had a little space underneath one of the bunks where we usually stored some things. He said he could sleep there, so we took him.

He had lost his arm and had a hook. I didn't want to take him. We didn't like to take anybody extra, especially a guy with a hook. I was worried about what could happen. But he insisted, so we let him come. I told him, "Now look. Don't you touch that net with that hook because if you go overboard with your hook caught in the net, you can't break that linen and only Christ could save you. If you want to help or do anything, just use your good hand and put your other one behind your back."

One night he got drunk downtown and walked down the street bashing a bunch of parking meters, breaking one after another with his hook. So they threw him in jail. A group of us fishermen took up a collection for his bail. We had enough money to pay for the damage to the parking meters, so we got him out of jail.

Another time he was driving taxi. He and his partner were each in their taxis and were racing down the middle of Astoria at two in the morning. He went over a bank and wrecked the cab. It was really a funny incident.

He was something, that fellow. He went places in the fishing business. He could catch fish, so he had a good reputation and got to run the big boats as long as he was alive.

He got a chance to run a king crab boat, a 165-footer out of Seattle. He was just a kid, but was a real go-getter, a good little fisherman. He figured if the Norwegians could fish in heavy weather, so could he, and he set out to prove it. He took this big boat up to the Bering Sea and anchored up in the bay. Some Japanese boats came in to get out of the weather, but he didn't want them there, so he threatened to ram them. That cost him his job.

Later he was running the *Thelma II* off Crescent City. He anchored up in Crescent City Bay. A storm was blowing. This is an open bay to the southeast, but that was the way the wind was blowing. He came on the radio laughing. He said he was anchored up in the bay and was taking waves over the bow. Then he signed off.

The next day we heard him on the radio again. He told us, "These Coast Guard men don't know how to get a boat off the beach." He was a sound sleeper. The anchor line broke and he didn't realize it and the boat was on the beach before he woke up. He lost the boat.

Later he had a chance to run the *Ida Mae*, my brother's boat. Jack, my brother, had sold it to the New England Fish Company. They had asked Jackie to run it. He went out one foggy morning, and hit the North Jetty of the Columbia. He was running full speed. That boat

My brother, Jack, in 1942.

opened up and sank right there. The crew jumped overboard and had to swim for it. But they got off okay.

He got the chance to run the 70-foot *Honey Bee*. He was laying out King Crab pots in Bristol Bay. He didn't like the way the crew was doing it, so he went back there to show them how it was done. These pots were eight feet by eight feet and about two and a half feet deep. He threw one overboard and he went right with it. He got his hook caught in the mesh of the pot, went overboard and he lost his life. All they got back was the hook. So it was his hook that finally got him. I was always afraid of that.

〜

I didn't see my brother Jack much after he left home. He went to live with a friend of his and got a job on some good salmon purse seiners in Alaska. He then got a crab boat, moved to Everett, Washington, and, following in our dad's footsteps, went into the crab business. He spent some time fishing on drag boats, for a while fishing with me (1942). He bought into a drag boat called *Ida Mae*. But most of the time he has been a crab fisherman. In Everett he had a pickup truck painted on the side, *J. M., The Crab King!* Most people around Everett know Jack with that label.

CHAPTER 12

Fish Stories

In the late forties we were dragging near the lightship. I had a partnership in the *Coolidge II*, skippered by Walt Miner. He was down around Tillamook. I got into a lot of big English sole. We had the whole deck loaded with English. I had never had fishing like this. I called my partner. I didn't want to tell him on the radio that we had a lot of fish because then every boat in the area would come, so I told Walt I needed an electric drill that he had on his boat to fix my drag doors.

In a couple of hours he showed up. He had that drill all wrapped up in oilskins and tied up with rope so he could throw it to us and we could pull it over. You can't get too close to each other at sea because you'd bump each other and do a lot of damage to both boats. Then I told him that I didn't need a drill at all. I just wanted to get him up there so he could get in on some of this great fishing. We sure had a good day, but the next morning there was no sign of any English. They had just disappeared.

≈

There was a guy fishing out of the Columbia on the *Ida Mae*. He was a little reckless with the truth about how much fish he caught. He'd come on the radio and talk about how much he had caught but then when he unloaded they just weren't there. Other guys would comment about how much fish this guy caught, and I would tell them, "Well, I'll tell you something. If you cut it in half and divide by two, you'll be doggone close to what he really has." I always did the opposite. I had the habit of underestimating my trips so I could feel better about what I actually ended up having. I think it worked out better that way.

⌐

We were dragging and getting a lot of female crab, so we were throwing them overboard when a Coast Guard boat came up to us. They launched a little boat and headed over to our boat. One of them hollered to us that they were coming aboard and not to throw anything overboard. So we stopped throwing crabs overboard. They were on a halibut patrol and were checking to see if we had any halibut because it was illegal to catch them in a drag net. This guy came on board. He was all dressed up in a suit. He told me to open the hatch so he could look down into the fish hold. He wasn't about to climb down there, with slime from the fish dripping down from the hatch combings. He should have been dressed in oilskins. If we ever did get any halibut we would bring it in and give it away or take it home for our personal use, but we weren't even supposed to do that. One of the inspectors told us if he caught us with any, even in the refrigerator, they would pinch us. They didn't come down and look very often, but they were on this duty and had to look like they were doing their job. So we gave him a few crabs to eat and he took off and went back to the ship.

⌐

We were sharking with the *Coolidge II* about ten to fifteen miles off Tillamook Rock. We had laid out our nets, which were floating nets, held up with glass balls. The soupfins are both on the bottom and on the top. We had to have our nets about fifty feet below the surface so the ships could pass by and not get the net caught in their propellers. Today they call this kind of net "the curtain of death." The Japanese use them a lot. They could have as much as twenty to thirty miles of fine filament nylon net out in the middle of the ocean and they take everything that came along. We used cotton nets. We were only after soupfin shark. It wouldn't have done us any good to get any other kind of shark because we couldn't sell it. This time when we brought in our nets, we couldn't believe all the sharks. I had never seen so many in my whole life. We had blue sharks, soupfin sharks, basking sharks, thresher sharks. You name it, we had it. They were all there. We had them, but we couldn't sell them. We had a big basking shark and had to cut him out of the net because he was so big and heavy. There was no way we could pick him up.

⌐

We used to fish a lot at Willapa Deep. It was about a four-hour run off the Washington Coast. There is a lot of petrale and dover sole there. We usually fished around the clock. It is deep there and you get just as much fish at night as you do during the day. In shallow water, sixty fathom or less, you only get junk at night, so we didn't bother. But in Willapa Deep, it is different. We would fish for a while, then drift for a few hours and try to get as much sleep as we could, and then we'd go back at it.

⌐

It never happened to me, but some of the boats would get big rocks in their nets out there, and they couldn't get the net up because they would be so heavy. So the only thing to do is to get the doors back and hook them up to the boat while the net was still hooked on the rock. It was common to hear a fisherman on the radio saying he was going to tow a rock to the beach. But even if you could do it, it would take maybe six hours or more to get there. Sometimes with the rock dragging along the bottom, it would wear a hole in the net and drop out. But sometimes they'd have to go all the way in. If a storm would come up while they were dragging a rock to the beach, they would be in real trouble. The only thing they could do would be to cut the net and get themselves in out of the weather.

⌐

Tuna boats have good radios because they talk long distances and tell each other where the fish are and keep in touch with each other. Two guys were fishing tuna. They were only a few miles apart, but these two were on the radio for fifteen or twenty minutes, just blabbering on about nothing. You're supposed to talk a maximum of five minutes so the channels are free for others to talk, but these guys didn't seem to care about anybody else. They had such powerful equipment, they could always hear each other and nobody else could drown them out. There was another fisherman who was trying to get on the radio, but couldn't. He had to wait until these two guys got through talking. When he did get on the air he was really disgusted and said, "If you want to talk so much, why don't you two get on the same boat?" I thought that was a great comment. He was right!

Someone was stove-piping shark livers. They are stored in five-gallon cans, each holding forty pounds. They are frozen at the fish plant. To test the quality of the livers, the round top is taken off the cans and a hole is drilled down the middle. Then they catch the shavings from this drill and take it to the lab and test it. That's the way they determined the value of the livers and then they gave you a certificate to put on the can. That way, when someone bought a can of livers, they knew the quality.

One of the fishermen tried to outsmart the system. He got a stovepipe a little bit smaller than the liver can lid. The dark livers are more valuable than the lighter livers. So this guy put all the dark livers in the center of the pipe and the light livers around the outside. When he got the can full, he pulled the pipe out, sealed it and put it in the freezer. When the test was made and they drilled into the can, they got the good liver and gave a good price to the can. Those who did the testing got smart quickly though, and they started drilling five holes, so nobody could fool them anymore with stove-piping.

In 1965, we found new fishing grounds for ocean perch off the Oregon Coast. We were running and I was watching the fathometer. Suddenly I saw a big black spot on the screen. I got pretty excited because I knew that meant fish. Boy, did it ever! In our first tow we got fifty thousand pounds of perch. Before the day was over, we had 150 thousand pounds of fish on the boat. They filled the hatches and

One hour, 50,000-pound tow of Pacific Ocean perch off the Oregon Coast, March 1965.

were piled on the deck so the boat was nearly sinking. We ran into Astoria and pulled up to Sebastian Stuart Fish Company. The manager came out and was really upset. He asked why we had not called in and told him we were coming. He said he couldn't possibly sell that much fish. It would have to go for mink feed. I hadn't called because I knew he would tell me not to bring it in. And I figured if I was there, he would have to deal with the fish. He got on the phone and sold it all. We got five cents a pound for it. That was the biggest catch of fish I ever made in one day.

I was fishing for shrimp off the Washington Coast for a Westport shrimp plant. It was the first plant to get a shrimp peeling machine from the Gulf. These Pacific Coast shrimp are very small (150 or more per pound in the round). It is impossible to peel them by hand. But this plant, using the peeling machine, canned the shrimp in half-pound cans and sold them as soon as they were canned. It seemed to me a good business to get in to.

Joe Anderson had a small custom salmon cannery for sport fishermen, located in an old leased plant that would be ideal for shrimp. It was in Warrenton, Oregon. I talked Joe into it and in 1957 we began the Pacific Shrimp, Incorporated. I was the president, Bud Conger Jr. was the secretary, and Joe was the manager. It was tough getting started. Draggers made more money dragging than they did shrimping, so it was hard to get boats to fish shrimp.

We ordered a shrimp-peeling machine on lease and got started. Another cannery that had been canning clams started to get into the shrimp business also. We had a hard time getting boats to fish for us since shrimp were hard to find, and we were only paying seven cents a pound. So boats did a lot of switching between shrimp and bottom fish, depending on where they could make the most money.

In 1966 things were really tough. Our plant manager was my brother-in-law, Ken Berg. We weren't even making enough to pay his salary, so Ken resigned from our plant and went to Kodiak, Alaska, to run a plant for a Mr. Bendikson. While Ken was there, a boat belonging to the cannery came in with some bad shrimp. Ken refused to can them. Since that was a big decision and the skipper was upset, Ken called Mr. Bendikson, who was in New York on

Cod end full of shrimp.

business, to tell him about the situation. He liked what Ken did and asked him to stay in Kodiak to run his cannery. But Ken had money invested in our cannery and wasn't happy being away from his family, so he came back to run the cannery in Warrenton.

One of the problems was our overhead. We found out that the shrimp-peeling machine company was charging the West Coast shrimp packers double the lease rate of the Gulf packers. So the West Coast shrimp packers got together and filed a class action suit against the peeler company.

It was a big trial held in Tacoma. I was president of Pacific Shrimp and had to testify as one of ten packers affected by the price fixing. The defense attorney asked all the fish packers how they got started in the shrimp business. He asked if we had read the Fish and Wildlife report of the shrimp caught on the West Coast. They all said yes. When they came to me, I told him that I had been in the business a long time and knew all about the amount of shrimp in these waters and I hadn't gone into the business blindfolded like the others.

Our attorney told us a lawsuit is like a horse race. You are not sure who is going to win until it is done. The case went on for some time. They asked me a lot of questions I couldn't answer because I didn't have some of the knowledge Ken Berg, our manager, had. So they put him on the stand to answer the business questions. When the case was over, our attorneys told me I won the case for them. I was a fisherman and knew the situation.

We got $25,000 for a settlement, which helped us out of our financial dilemma. I was president of the company for twenty-two years, and Ken was our CEO for twenty-one years. We finally sold out and the new buyers went broke in a few years. Because they still owed us the money from the sale, even after a long hassle, we ended up getting only about a third of the selling price.

CHAPTER 13

A Risky Business

There's a lot of danger involved in the fishing business. Sometimes you're drifting out there and not at anchor. You have your mast light on in the middle of the night and ships are running up and down the coast and you never know what you're going to run in to.

⤳

I was dragging off the Columbia and I heard a fellow come on the radio and say, "The *Coho* shot me." And then he signed off. There was no indication where the call came from. I think somewhere near San Francisco. Then we heard the Coast Guard went out and found the *Coho,* arrested the man, and towed the boat to San Francisco. The skipper was left on board to steer. When they got to San Francisco, there wasn't anybody on the boat. He must have jumped overboard on the way in. If he shot the other guy, he may have figured it would be the end of him anyway.

⤳

In 1944 there was a big tuna run in Astoria. A lot of the boats put bait tanks on board and went fishing with hook and line. Howard Bronson had the *Zarembo III.* He was in the shipyard and had his bait tank full of water and was testing his equipment. One of the yard superintendents went aboard and the boat went down about an inch or so just with his own weight. So he told the skipper the boat wasn't seaworthy. Bronson had been running the boat in rough weather, dragging out around Cape Flattery, and he didn't believe it wasn't seaworthy. So he left the dock and went out fishing. And that was the last anybody ever heard of him. It is likely he turned over out at sea. The superintendent knew more about it than he did, but he didn't take his advice and he lost the boat and his life.

↬

The *Dorothy Joan* was out of Seattle. It was fishing tuna with a bait tank, too. They found a bunch of debris floating in the water the next morning, which was the only thing left of her.

↬

The insurance companies started getting pretty strict because lots of boats with bait tanks were sinking. So they started giving stability tests. It saved a lot of boat loss. Fishermen don't know how to assess this very well, and don't know much about top heaviness. It takes a naval architect to figure that out. So the insurance companies came up with a lot of new rules and regulations before they would insure the tuna boats.

↬

A friend of mine was in the Shelikof Straits by Kodiak Island. It was freezing and the weather was so rough he decided to turn around and go back, but he never made it. He got in a trough and the boat turned over. The boat was lost and everyone aboard.

↬

It happened quite a bit. The boats would put on two reels, one on top of the other, and they put on their nets. It was deceiving. These were big boats and it looked like they could handle it, but if a boat gets in a trough and it gets rough and the fish in the hold shift, the boat can just roll over.

↬

Off the Washington Coast the *Owner's Joy* was dragging for shrimp. A boat came out of the river heading for the tuna grounds, and it headed straight for the *Owner's Joy*. He figured the boat was just coming out to see him, maybe watch him pull up the net so he could see what he was catching. But the guy got closer and closer and he wasn't slowing down and pretty soon, BOOM! He hit him right midship, full speed. He broke three planks eight inches above the water line on up to the deck. If he had broken it below the waterline, it would have sunk him right away. He was lucky that he took the hit near midship, right near a bulkhead, because the boat is pretty strong there. The guy in the boat that hit him was sound asleep. He had probably had the boat on the automatic pilot.

~

I was running the *New Hope* in the fifties off the Oregon Coast. We were working back in the stern with the boat turning gradually. Nobody was on the wheel. We thought we had it straight ahead, but it was gradually turning around. One of the cables didn't clear the stern and came off the edge of the boat when it turned. The stanchions, where the blocks are, were too far forward. We put them forward so the boat will turn better when we're dragging. When that cable slipped off the corner of the stern, it straightened out and hit me right in the chest. It knocked me right off my feet. I was lucky it didn't knock me overboard or cut me in half. It the boat had turned more, it probably would have. I was really scared, but it didn't injure me. So I was lucky. The ocean is a big place and if you get into trouble, there isn't anybody around since the boats are scattered here and there.

~

There was a drag boat out of Newport that was supposed to come in on a Monday. It didn't come in. So the fishermen's wives called the Coast Guard. They went out to search, and found them way off shore. The boat was idling in the water. Both of the guys were tangled up in the net reel on the stern. One of them was dead. The other guy was alive but was apparently trying to get his partner out of the reel when he got caught too. The controls were out of reach on the other side of the boat. The only thing that saved the one guy is that the boat was turning slowly in a big circle. It got up into the wind and the wind was blowing harder than the boat was going ahead. So the wind blew the boat backwards and the cod end got caught in the wheel and stopped the engine. If it wasn't for that, they both would have been wrapped up badly in the reel. I never heard if the one guy made it. He was injured very badly. That was about the worst tragedy I've heard in the fishing industry outside of the loss of life altogether.

A Russian side trawler off the Washington Coast.

In 1968 I was invited to go on a Russian trawler. There was a group of Russian ships fishing off the Washington Coast. I went with several Coast Guard people, some Fish and Wildlife personnel, and an interpreter from the University of Washington. I was the only fisherman there. Dr. Harvey from the Astoria Seafood Lab had made the arrangements. We used the 80-foot *John N. Cobb* as our research vessel. We went about forty miles offshore to get to the Russian fleet. Then we boarded a 275-foot stern ramp trawler with over a hundred people on board. We stayed on board about four hours, observing their operation. They processed the fish they caught all in the same day. Most of what they caught was hake. We can't use hake because they are so perishable and wouldn't keep until we got them back to our on-shore processors. Their first drag that day they tore their net up, so we didn't see their whole process, but we got a tour of the ship. We saw all their navigation equipment but were not allowed to see the radio room. We stayed for dinner on the ship, which was served with lots of vodka. There was one woman on board. She waited on tables for dinner.

Later we were going to Seattle with the *New Hope* and stopped by two factory ships. First we traded American cigarettes and coins. Then we threw a knife up on the deck. It caused quite a commotion. The officer of the ship grabbed the knife and took it away immediately. We went on to Seattle.

⌐

I recently heard of two boats that were lost. The *Kodiak* was lost on Tillamook Bar. I think he took a breaker and everyone was lost. A new boat out of San Francisco was coming into the Columbia River Bar with forty-five thousand pounds of bottom fish and we never heard from him again. Sometimes fishermen try to cut the spit short to save time. They don't go around buoy No. 1 at Peacock Spit. They take a chance and go in closer to the breakers. A big sneaker can come in and that's all it takes.

⌐

One time in the forties we had been fishing sharks with the *Elector* and were coming in over the bar. There was a big sea running but we wanted to get in before the storm came. The tide was just starting to ebb. I was on top of the house and I saw this big breaker coming. I quickly slowed the engine down and took it out of gear so we wouldn't go too fast. We took that break. It could have taken the house right off and that would have been the end of us, but we took this break and went down on the break just like a surfboard. When she broke, there was white water all over. I put it back in gear, put the clutch in, turned the propeller and nothing happened. I thought we must have lost the wheel because we weren't going anywhere. But in a couple minutes that foam went away and we got into solid water and, by golly, the wheel took hold and we got inside. That was close because if we had broken down there, we would have drifted back and we would have taken other breakers because the tide was ebbing and we were right on the bar. Rocco Danielovich was my deck hand and cook, and was down below. He told me later it felt as though the boat was on wheels, like a wagon going down a pebble stone street. The boat just shook! That was the only break I took on the Columbia River bar in all the years I was fishing around the Columbia. I never want to go through that again.

⌐

One time we were running out to the fishing grounds and I was trying to get some sleep on the way out. A fellow named Francis Banich was at the wheel. All of a sudden I felt the boat slow down and I knew something was wrong and I jumped out of the bunk and ran up to the wheel. It was about midnight and I saw this other boat with his floodlights on, and he was so close to us I could have jumped from my boat to his. We missed him by inches. Francis stuttered and he was so scared he couldn't say a word. It was a full five minutes before he could say anything. I kept asking him what happened. Finally he told me he didn't really know. They were going around in circles so he got their running lights mixed up and didn't know which way they were going. I had seen the name of the boat, so I called the skipper in the morning and asked who was at the wheel. He told me the cook was. That's when I told him that I almost cut him in half. I was so scared that I just shook when I was telling him about it.

We were in Mexico, fishing on the *King Fisher*. We were up on the inside of the Baja tip around Cabo San Lucas. It was a nice calm day, but really hot, so the guys started jumping off the boat to go swimming. One guy was up on top of the mast. All of a sudden he started yelling for everyone to get out of the water quick! He could see some hammerhead sharks coming. And boy we got out of the water in a hurry. Because the water is so warm, there are lots of sharks in those waters. I really don't know what they would do to a person, but I wouldn't want to be in the water to find out. It was really good the guy was on the mast to see them coming.

On this same trip I was at the wheel. There was always one guy at the wheel when the others went down to eat dinner. Then someone would then relieve the guy at the wheel so he could eat. The cook always saved him something and kept it hot. When I was relieved at the wheel, I went down to the galley. The cook had made up some *pasta e fagioli*, a Slav dish of beans and macaroni. I didn't pay too much attention to what was going on. Everybody was sitting around when I started to eat. One guy said, "I wouldn't eat those if I were you." I looked around and there were all these plates sitting there full of beans. Then they told me the beans were full of bugs. Every bean had a worm in it. So we had to throw the whole thing out. I probably would have eaten them if he hadn't told me. I don't care much about beans anyway. I was mostly eating the macaroni, but I didn't eat any more.

⌒

One time we were coming in from Willapa Deep. It was night. The cook told me he would take the wheel for a while so I could sleep. Usually when I am out fishing, I don't trust many people. But I figured if we were three hours off the beach, then I could set the alarm for two-and-a-half hours, and we'd still be half an hour off the beach if we were in trouble. I woke up in a couple of hours and came up to the wheel and here was the cook, sound asleep and heading straight for Peacock Spit. I just took the wheel, woke him up and told him to go down and get some sleep. I didn't want to bawl him out or anything because he did give me a chance to sleep. So, he went down and I took her in. If I hadn't gotten up, we probably would have lost the boat.

⌒

I was running the *Kathy Jo* and we were going down river on an ebb tide. We got down near Lower Sands and I heard the engine start to slow down. I knew we were in trouble. I turned up river and tried to get up as far as I could in a little deeper water so I could throw the hook. Then we could go down and see what was going on with the engine. I turned the brake loose on the anchor winch. The anchor weighed between five-to six-hundred pounds, but it didn't drop. We don't use the anchor very much. When we are out fishing we are either running or we drift. We almost never drop the hook or use the anchor winch.

I told one of the crew to go get a twenty-pound sledge and I took a big swing, hit it and she dropped. We got anchored up and we were safe. If you are drifting in the river with no anchor and the engine stops, you're in really big trouble. You don't know where you'll end up. So I was really scared until that anchor dropped. It ended up not being a big problem. One of our fuel tanks was out of fuel and we had to switch tanks.

⌒

In 1944 we were sharking north of the Farallon Islands. We were running into San Francisco in a thick fog, and we didn't have any radar, just a compass. We heard a ship's horn and we blew our horn. This kept up but we were getting closer and closer to each other. All of a sudden the fog opened up a little bit and we saw this Navy ship going into San Francisco. By then we were backing up at full speed, but we still almost collided. It was real close and very scary. It really gets a guy wondering, especially in bad or foggy weather.

⌐

The *Fearless* was dragging out of Warrenton for the San Juan Fish Company. They were around Tillamook Rock heading for Astoria when a storm came up. He got on the radio and said he was taking water over the stern. The wind was blowing hard and he was going with the wind so the seas were piling up on his stern. He had a particularly low stern because it was a former tugboat. It had a double house on it. He called and called. The *Rose Ann* was near the lightship and heard him. He asked them to call the Coast Guard and tell them he was sinking, that the water was coming in the engine room. Then he asked the skipper of the *Rose Ann* if he would call his wife and tell her he didn't know whether he would make it but he had $10,000 of life insurance.

The *Rose Ann* relayed the message to the Coast Guard, and then we heard the *Rose Ann's* skipper on the radio say, "Here comes a big one." And that was the last we heard of the *Rose Ann*. The crew and the boat were all lost. But the *Fearless* made it through somehow.

⌐

When the Japanese bombed Pearl Harbor, we were listening to the radio and the first announcement was that Gray's Harbor was bombed. That really scared us because Gray's Harbor was really close to us. If they bombed Gray's Harbor, we'd be in big trouble. So everyone in Astoria was pretty scared for a while.

During the war there were nets across the river to prevent a submarine from coming into the river. The fishermen were supposed to come into the river before it got dark. They had a scow anchored down at the mouth of the river and we'd have to report. Then we'd go through a passage between the submarine nets. They could close it at any time they needed to, but it was a way the ships could come and go in the river.

⌐

They also blacked out Astoria because they were afraid of bombing of the mainland. During the blackouts, they shut the lights down and everything was dark. The only light was from the buoys flashing in the river.

⌐

We were dragging near North Head at the extreme southwest corner of Washington, at the mouth of the Columbia River. After a long day of fishing, we were anchored in about twenty fathom of water not far from North Head. It was about midnight. I was out on the deck when I saw a Japanese submarine surface between my boat and the shore. This was about the time there had been some shelling of the coast near Warrenton, Oregon. The sub was running on the surface, going up the coast. Five minutes after it went by, a searchlight came on from North Head, but it was too late for them to see the sub. It was exciting but pretty frightening.

Captain Moskovita at the wheel of the *Rodema* watching the fathometer.

CHAPTER 14

A Good Ending

My girlfriend in 1942, who capped those empty quart beer bottles to be used for floats on the shark nets, became my wife. June Berg and I got married on August 20, 1943. We bought a house in Williamsport, a suburb of Astoria. We had four girls, Georgene, Joy, Jo Ann, and Kathleen. June did most of the work in raising the girls because I was at sea most of the time and wasn't able to spend much time with the four girls. It was one of the problems of being a commercial fisherman.

George and June on their wedding day, 1943.

In 1976 June and I bought a gillnet boat up in Puget Sound, a 37-foot wood boat. I bought the boat with a partner, and we fished together for a year, and then he sold his interest to me. For a year in 1977–1978 my daughter Kathy fished with me. Then for about eight years, from 1978–1986 June fished with me for sockeye salmon. Most of the time we fished around the Point Roberts area right on the Canadian border where most of the seine boats and gillnetters worked. Being Norwegian, she had fishing in her blood and made a good boat puller. It was awfully nice to have your cook aboard as well.

⤙

In 1980 while gillnetting for salmon in the Sound, not far from Birch Bay, we got into a lot of huge dogfish drifting over Alden Bank. They came in so fast we could have loaded the boat. I took them out of the net but more came in as fast as I could take them out. I have never seen so many that big. I wore myself out just taking the dogfish out of the net.

⤙

We just got through picking up our gillnet and started to run toward Blaine when the engine slowed down for no reason. There was a lot of noise in the propeller area. We slowed to a crawl and I called the Coast Guard for help. I couldn't steer with the rudder, and I had to steer with a pole and a bucket over the side of the boat. I kept looking for the Coast Guard to come from the direction of Bellingham. But pretty soon a hovercraft came from the Canada side. I had never seen a boat like this before. This was a $1.5 million outfit. They came alongside the boat, put a line on us and towed us to the harbor in Blaine. We put the boat on dry dock and discovered the copper ground plate for the radio telephone had come loose from the hull and had become tangled in the propeller and rudder. It was about one-sixteenth of an inch thick and about four by eight feet.

⤙

One night we made two sets for salmon and had $10,000 worth of fish in one night. We were getting $2.20 a pound and each fish weighed between 5.5 to 6 pounds. That runs into big money. I couldn't believe it. The law was that you had to have your nets picked up and on the boat by nine in the morning. At noon we

Daughters Georgene, Jo
Ann, Kathleen, and Joy
(clockwise from left), 1958

were still picking fish out of our net, and an airplane flew overhead. They landed, although they couldn't come aboard because it was too choppy. But he yelled over to us, "You're way overtime!" I told them I knew that but there wasn't anything we could do because we had so many fish and it took so much time to get them out. They couldn't hear me very well so they flew to shore and got a speedboat and came out to the boat and boarded. I was tired after working so hard to get all those fish, so I had gone down to the bunk and had gone to sleep. The Fish and Wildlife people came aboard and took a picture of me lying in the bunk. They said, "We're not going to cite you, but we are going to turn this over to the district attorney for fishing overtime." I told them it couldn't be helped because we had to get the fish out and get the net in before we drifted across the Canadian border. He said a lot of boats that night had gotten a lot of fish and were overtime too. So, it all depends on the situation. Well, they left and that was the last I ever heard of it. That was also the only really good fishing we had in all the eight to ten years we fished up there. The rest of the time it was scratching for whatever we got. That one night was good and we sure enjoyed it.

In 1983, we were fishing around the Seattle area by the Kingston ferry. It was right where the ferry goes across to Kingston from the mainland there at Edmonds. I laid my net out near another gill-netter one night just before dark. I had just got my net out when a guy came up to me and said, "Hey, you pick that net up. You're too damn close to me. If you don't pick up, I'll ram you. Normally I would have argued with him, but with June along, I didn't want to do that, so we picked up and beat it. But, that's how they were down there. Some of them get on drugs and you never know what they are going to do. We headed back to Bellingham. Around midnight we got to Bellingham Bay and I thought I would lay the net out. I threw the ball right next to the shore so no fish could get between the end of the net and the beach. The wind was blowing and I was drifting out from the shore. The net was kind of tangled and I was in a big hurry to get it untangled and overboard before I got too far away from the beach. Suddenly I lost my breath. I had to stop and sit down. I knew there was something wrong.

So we went in and I went to the doctor. They took a lot of tests and sent me to Virginia Mason Hospital in Seattle. They put some dye in my veins and then took x-rays and said, "You're blocked up 100 percent in one vein and 95 percent in another and 50 percent in a third. You're due for a heart bypass." I said, "Well I can't do it now. We have to go to Astoria and pay bills and this and that." They gave me some nitroglycerin pills to take along and told me if I had any problems, to take a pill. So we went, but I didn't have any problems.

About a week later they set up a date and I went to have the bypass. After the operation was over, they came out and talked to June and my daughter, Gerogene, who had come out from Colorado for the operation. They said, "Well, it is over, but, if he comes out of it he may be a vegetable and he may not come out of it at all." Boy, those are scary words. Man! I was in intensive care for a week. They gave me the wrong anesthetic (at least it didn't work on me), so I wasn't getting oxygen to the brain during part of the operation. They were really worried about it. But I did come out of it, and I am not a vegetable, and I'm still here, thirteen years later.

I knew they had taken veins out of my legs to do the bypass, so later I asked my doctor how those veins looked that he used. He

Our gillnetter, *Janeth*, used to fish sockeye salmon in the Puget Sound for ten years.

said, "Well, I'd give them a grade of C. Pretty average." But that's what they had to use. All this time though, I haven't lost my breath or had any pains in my heart or chest or anything. Of course, I never did have any pains. I just lost my breath. It makes me wonder if I even needed that bypass. But anyway, they did it and I'm still here. I don't think those bypasses last more than ten years before they go to pot again. I hope I don't have any more trouble.

June and I gillnetted in Puget Sound a few more years before we quit in 1986. My knee triggered on me and I fell. It was like an electric shock in my knee. I figured Somebody was telling me something. I might be walking around the gillnet boat to go drop the hook and my knee could trigger again and I'd go overboard. So I thought I'd better quit fishing altogether and I have been ashore ever since.

⌐

There have been so many changes in the bottom fish industry since I began fishing off the Columbia River in 1939. When I started, things were pretty primitive. We didn't have cable or cable winches. I used old manila purse lines spliced together to let down the doors to the bottom. Then we pulled the net and doors in on a gypsy head. We only had twenty-five fathom of line from the doors to the net. We would back the boat up and then pull in the slack line by hand.

Then we pulled the net up to the top of the boom until we got to the cod end that was laced up. We opened it up and brailed the fish out with a brailer hoop about three feet in diameter. We didn't know anything about a splitting strap then.

What was really lacking were all the electronics fishermen have now. To determine how deep the water was, we used a sounding lead tied to the end of a spool of wire marked every five fathom.

We didn't have a radio telephone. We had a regular car radio we used to hear the news and weather.

We finally leased a flash-type fathometer for $45 a month. Then came the Direction Finder, Loran, and Radio telephones so we could talk to other boats and to shore. Next came a paper sounding machine that showed fish on the bottom. Then came radar and the automatic pilot to steer the boat. More recently there are pieces of electronic gear to allow the fisherman to see fish actually going into the net, allowing the skipper to see where he has been, where he is going, and how much fish is already in the net.

When we fished we probably dumped 50 percent of the fish overboard because they were too small to fillet. We used four- to five-inch mesh. Now there are big fishing vessels up to three hundred feet long that are fish processor-type ships that fish around the clock and take everything they get.

An important advancement in the bottom fishing industry was the midwater trawl and the new-type drag door that spreads the net. This new midwater trawl came from Europe with big reels that wind up the trawl net. The entrance to the trawl is about a hundred feet high and about two hundred feet wide. A whole house could fit in the entrance of it. It takes alot of horsepower to pull this trawl. The large entrance to the net is what catches the fish. The mesh size in some of these big trawls are up to two hundred feet in size and taper down to a small mesh that the fish can't get through, then on into the cod end. The big trawls are pulled up the stern ramp and are unloaded from the top down to the cod end bottom. They have zippers from the top of the cod to the bottom in about five-thousand-pound sections. The fish are washed out of the top of the cod end with a water hose into the manhole plate where they are stored. Then the net is rolled into the next section, a very simple procedure. Four men can handle the whole operation.

If the hake plant the government built in 1966 in Aberdeen, Washington had the midwater trawls they have today, it would have been a big success making fish flour to feed the hungry of the world. Back then they couldn't catch enough hake to keep the plant going. After a few years they junked the plant.

↜

Factory trawlers were another advancement. There are about sixty of them working in Bristol Bay, Alaska over to the Russian border. They have stern ramps on these trawlers. The cod end would be hanging over the stern ramp and is pulled in as the top of the cod end is unloaded. The cod end would be longer than half the size of the boat. They fish around the clock. These factory trawlers have around a hundred people aboard to process fish in about twenty-four hours. The pollock caught in Alaska is processed frozen and stored on the vessel until delivered. The frozen fish are used to make food products they use in Japan and other countries. Imitation crab-meat sells for about one fourth the price of King Crab meat and is a good seller.

These factory trawlers come down to the California, Oregon, and Washington coasts after finishing the season in Alaska. They fish for hake on the Pacific Coast and the fish are used for the same purpose. When I caught hake, we couldn't sell it. It was a poor keeper and couldn't be iced for over one day.

The fish don't have a chance to survive with this kind of new gear. I predict bottom trawling will be outlawed altogether and replaced with hook and line with baited hooks and bottom pots. We're seeing boats being put on a quota and government buy-back programs in an attempt to save the fishery.

↜

I don't really miss the fishing. It was a nice way to make a living, you know, but nowadays it's really dog-eat-dog—a lot of competition and lots of headaches involved with the fishing business. I am glad to be out of it. But I was in it a long time and I have a lot of memories of all the things that happened. It has been quite a life. And that's the way it was.

George and June Moskovita in 1985.

APPENDIX
George's Boats

While George Moskovita is undoubtedly the star of his memoir, he had a strong supporting cast with the many boats that he either owned, operated, rebuilt, or sank during his fifty-year career. In a 1994 interview published in the *Fisherman's News*, George said that he had owned sixteen different boats.[1]

The *Elector* was a 56-foot limit seiner, owned by Dome Moskovita, who fished it for salmon in Bellingham Bay, and for dragging out of Astoria. George told the *Fisherman's News* that it was built in 1914 for the Bellingham Canning Company at the Barbare Brothers Shipyard in Tacoma. It originally had a 40 hp Frisco Standard gasoline engine, replaced by a DC3000 Cat in 1943, and new bulwarks. It was later sold to Tony Skrivinich of Gig Harbor and it was still in operation in 1994, according to George in his 1994 interview. In 1930, when George was seventeen, he went to Alaska to fish for salmon on the *Elector*.

Dome Moskovita built the 56-foot *New Zealand* in 1931 at the Barbee Shipyard in Seattle, with a 75 hp Atlas Imperial diesel. Dome brought her to Astoria in 1939 and helped to start the drag fishery. Sold and renamed the *Good Tidings*, she floundered in the Peril Strait, Alaska, in the 1970s, and sank. It was "a very nice boat," George recalled to the *Fisherman's News* in 1994.

In 1936, George went to San Pedro to fish for sardines on the *Lansing*.

He also fished for tuna off Mexico on the *Kingfisher*. He went back to sardine fishing on the *Farallon* in 1937. Around this same time, Dome brought the *New Zealand* to San Pedro to fish for mackerel.

George bought the *Treo* in 1940 and it sank on the Columbia River bar. George went back to California to fish for sardines and tuna, on the *Western Star*. He also fished for sardines on the *Sunlight* off San Francisco. He later ran the *Muzon* out of Astoria.

George returned to Bellingham in 1942 and went into partnership with his father on the *Elector*, which he rigged for shark fishing out of Astoria.

He bought the *Coolidge II* in 1944 and it had his first diesel engine.

George went back to California in 1950 and saw the partially de-stroyed *El Padre*, an 82-foot seiner, in a shipyard. He found the *Esperia III*, a boat that had sunk, but its pilothouse was not dam-aged. George combined the parts of the two boats and named the combined vessel the *Joy M*, after his daughter.

He bought another burned boat, the *Aurora*, for $1,850. It was 85 feet long with a 22-foot beam. He rebuilt it and named it the *Jo Ann*.

George bought the *Georgene M* in 1952 and named it after his oldest daughter. It was 65 feet long and went up on the beach near Point Arena. George, who was not onboard, bought the wreck from the insurance company for $500 and salvaged the engine.

He bought the *New Hope* in 1954. It was an 82-foot boat with a 21.5 foot beam and a Fairbanks engine. It is with the *New Hope* that George says he began his career of fishing and "salvaging boats on the side," (94). He paid $11,500 and it delivered the record 150,000-pound trip of Pacific Ocean perch to Astoria. It also sank in the boat basin at Astoria during Christmas of 1963.

The *Rodoma* came along in 1956, bought from Pan American Fisheries for $3,500. He owned the boat until 1968.

George was fishing on the *Mary R* in 1965 when it sank off Cape Disappointment, Washington. Nobody was hurt.

George bought a former minesweeper, the *Tidewater Shaver*, in 1967. He turned the 136-foot boat into the *Kathy Jo*, named after another daughter. He sold the boat to the Israel Love family, a Seattle-based urban commune that had, at its zenith, more than three hundred members. It was the *Kathy Jo* that trawled up the World War II un-exploded bomb.

He owned the *Eagle*, an 85-foot halibut schooner, bought for $8,500. He also owned a shrimper, the *Tide*, which sank off Cape Disappointment. George was not onboard.

George also had a tugboat, the *Arrow IV*, which had sunk in the Warrenton boat basin. He bought it for $2,600 and salvaged it and sold it to another fisherman.

He bought the *Taasinge* in 1981. It was a 68-foot shrimper and he bid $3,650 for it. He renamed it the *Four Daughters* and sold it for $45,000.

In 1985, George bought the *Angela Carol* for $95,000 from a credit union and was able to overhaul the engine and sell it again, making a profit of $24,000.

George's last boat was the *Janeth*, a 37-foot gillnetter that he and June fished out of Bellingham from 1978 until 1986, when they finally retired.